SCHOOL
OF THE
MIRACULOUS
STUDY GUIDE

STUDY GUIDE

SCHOOL
OF THE
MIRACULOUS

A PRACTICAL GUIDE TO WALKING IN DAILY MIRACLES

KYNAN BRIDGES

WHITAKER
HOUSE

Unless otherwise indicated, all Scripture quotations are taken from the *King James Version Easy Read Bible*, kjver®, © 2001, 2007, 2010, 2015 by Whitaker House. Used by permission. All rights reserved. Scripture quotations marked (niv) are taken from the *Holy Bible, New International Version*®, niv®, © 1973, 1978, 1984, 2011 by Biblica, Inc.® Used by permission of Zondervan. All rights reserved worldwide. www.zondervan.com. The "NIV" and "New International Version" are trademarks registered in the United States Patent and Trademark Office by Biblica, Inc.®

Boldface type in the Scripture quotations indicates the author's emphasis. The forms Lord and God (in small capital letters) in Bible quotations represent the Hebrew name for God *Yahweh* (Jehovah), while *Lord* and *God* normally represent the name *Adonai*, in accordance with the Bible version used.

Some definitions of Greek words are taken from the New Testament Greek Lexicon—King James Version, based on Thayer's and Smith's Bible Dictionary, plus others (public domain), www.BibleStudyTools.com. Some definitions of Hebrew words are taken from the Old Testament Hebrew Lexicon—King James Version or New American Standard, which is the Brown, Driver, Briggs, Gesenius Lexicon (public domain), BibleStudyTools.com. Other Greek and Hebrew definitions are taken from the resources of blueletterbible.org and the electronic version of *Strong's Exhaustive Concordance of the Bible*, strong, (© 1980, 1986, and assigned to World Bible Publishers, Inc. Used by permission. All rights reserved.).

Unless otherwise indicated, all dictionary definitions are taken from OxfordDictionairies.com, Oxford University Press, © 2019.

School of the Miraculous Study Guide:
A Practical Guide to Walking in Daily Miracles

Kynan Bridges Ministries, Inc.
P.O. Box 159
Ruskin, FL 33575
www.kynanbridges.com
info@kynanbridges.com

ISBN: 978-1-64123-564-8
eBook ISBN: 978-1-64123-565-5
Printed in the United States of America
© 2020 by Kynan Bridges

Whitaker House
1030 Hunt Valley Circle
New Kensington, PA 15068
www.whitakerhouse.com

1 2 3 4 5 6 7 8 9 10 11 ᴜᴊ 27 26 25 24 23 22 21 20

CONTENTS

HOW TO USE THIS STUDY GUIDE

Welcome to *School of the Miraculous Study Guide: A Practical Guide to Walking in Daily Miracles*. We are delighted that you have made the decision to dig deeper into God's Word. This study guide is designed as a stand-alone biblical study on the theme of the miraculous. The course may be completed independently by individual students or may be used in a group setting, such as a Bible study, a Sunday school class, a course on the foundations of the Christian faith, or a prayer group.

ELEMENTS OF EACH LESSON

Chapter Theme

The main idea of each chapter is summarized for emphasis and clarity.

Questions for Reflection

Thought questions are posed as a warm-up to lead into the study. (For group study, these questions may be asked before or after reading the "Chapter Theme," at the discretion of the leader.)

Exploring Principles and Purposes

Questions and review material are provided to summarize and highlight the principles and truths within each chapter and begin to lead the reader/group participant to personalize what is being studied. Page numbers from the *School of the Miraculous* book corresponding to the answers to each question are supplied for easy reference. (An answer key for the "Exploring Principles and Purposes" questions may be found on page 97.)

Conclusion

A summary or implication statement is included to put the theme of the chapter into perspective.

Applying Principles of the Miraculous

Thought-provoking questions and suggestions for personal action and prayer are provided to help the individual/group participant apply the study material to their particular life circumstances. This section includes three parts:

+ Thinking It Over

+ Acting on It

+ Praying About It

Miracle Testimony

Testimonies are included to give glory to God and encourage the reader to walk in the miraculous.

INTRODUCTION

When *School of the Miraculous* was published, I saw a tremendous response from people whenever I spoke about the book and its themes. Many people asked me if I had additional resources on the topic. This study guide was developed to help you plant the principles of the book deep into your heart and apply them to your circumstances so you can live a supernatural lifestyle.

As I wrote in the preface to the book, this work was born from my experiences over the years in talking with thousands of believers who were greatly discouraged and frustrated because they had heard about the power of God to meet their needs and the needs of those around them, but they weren't seeing its activity in their lives. Their inability to access God's power was leaving them without the help they desperately needed. The idea began to form in my mind of writing a handbook on walking in the miraculous—a "Miracles 101" course, a *School of the Miraculous*.

I hope you will enroll! I lay a strong biblical foundation for the present-day work and ministry of the Holy Spirit and share revelatory keys on how to live in the miraculous daily. The body of Christ lacks teaching on this vital topic, and I have designed these materials so that every believer can learn to operate according to God's power.

My goal is to demystify the process of receiving miracles. We often have the idea that a miracle is a rare event, but this is not a biblical perspective. We can identify specific spiritual steps that will free us and enable us to live daily in the miraculous, and I am passionate about walking you through each one. We will cover such topics as "Developing a Supernatural Culture," "Knowing Our Identity," "Breaking the Stronghold of Fear," "The Spirit of Awakening," "Everyday Miracles and the Power of Prayer," and "Five Keys to Activating God's Power." Throughout all the chapters of *School of the Miraculous*, you will discover how to experience the presence of God in your life, overcome spiritual roadblocks to victory, recognize and unlock the gifts of the Spirit, declare God's Word, and release His supernatural power.

When we develop an intimate relationship with God's Holy Spirit—the Miracle Worker—we will live in the power of the miraculous. I can confirm from my own life, and from the lives of many others, that "everyday" people can see God's miraculous power working on their behalf. In fact, I expect to see a miracle every day! I pray that this expectation will capture your heart, as well, and that you will begin to walk in the miraculous purposes that God has planned for you.

"EVERYDAY" PEOPLE CAN SEE THE MIRACULOUS POWER OF GOD WORKING ON THEIR BEHALF.

CHAPTER 1

GOD'S PURPOSE FOR MIRACLES

CHAPTER THEME

Everyday Christians around the world are seeing the miraculous power of God move in their lives—and the same can be true for you. It is happening because these believers have come into an awareness of the spiritual realm, and they have a lifestyle of walking in the Spirit, which gives them access to heaven's resources. We cannot access something if we are not aware of it! *But revelation releases miracles.* A renewed understanding of God's purposes will open the door to the miraculous in your life.

QUESTIONS FOR REFLECTION

+ What are your beliefs about miracles? Do you think the miraculous power of God is still at work today? Or do you perhaps believe miracles were only relevant during the first century when the church was being established? Please provide a reason for your answer.

+ Have you experienced the supernatural power of God firsthand or witnessed it in others' lives? If so, describe such an experience.

+ Do you want to see God's miraculous power manifest in your life? Why or why not?

EXPLORING PRINCIPLES AND PURPOSES

1. _____ releases miracles. (p. 17)

2. Why does God manifest His supernatural power? (p. 17)

   _____

   _____

   _____

   _____

   _____

3. Explain the experience of being "slain in the Spirit." (p. 16)

   _____

   _____

   _____

   _____

   _____

4. _____, _____, and _____ are God's signposts in the earthly realm. (p. 17)

5. In Mark 16:17, what does the word *"signs"* from the Greek term *sēmeion* mean? (pp. 17, 19)

   _____

   _____

   _____

   _____

   _____

6. What does the word *"follow"* from the Greek *parakoloutheō* mean? (p. 19)

_____

_____

_____

_____

7. God is a God of _____ and _____. (p. 19)

8. Many believers want to see miracles, but they fail to understand that miracles are conditional on implementing and responding to various divine systems. How does Matthew 6:33 guide us in activating miracles? (p. 19)

_____

_____

_____

_____

_____

9. What happened when Jesus preached the kingdom? (p. 19)

_____

_____

_____

_____

10. Signs and wonders are destined to _____ believers, not the other way around. (p. 20)

11. As we seek the kingdom of God and proclaim the gospel, at least four results will take place: (p. 20)

_____

_____

_____

_____

12. Explain the "gospel of exclusion." (p. 20)

_____

_____

_____

_____

_____

13. Complete the verse below, which shows God's desire to demonstrate His power in our lives in a tangible way. (p. 21)

    *"For the _____ of the LORD run to and fro throughout the whole _____,
    to show Himself _____ in the behalf of them whose _____ is
    _____ toward Him"* (2 Chronicles 16:9).

14. One of the Greek words translated "miracles" in the New Testament is *dunamis,* among whose meanings is "power for performing miracles." This is the term from which we derive the English word _____, which fittingly describes God's power! (p. 21)

15. When Jesus preached, there was demonstration. When the apostles preached, there was demonstration. When we preach, there should be _____! (p. 21)

16. The _____ _____ provides every believer with miracle power. (p. 22)

17. The _____ in the Holy Spirit is a key element in experiencing the miraculous power of God. (p. 22)

18. In the kingdom of God, faith is spelled R-I-S-K. Complete the meaning of the acronym: (p. 23)

    R_____ your faith for more.

    I_____ heaven by stepping out.

    S_____ on the Word of God.

    K_____ pressing until you see a miracle.

CONCLUSION

Every believer in Jesus can operate in the miraculous power of God daily. In fact, it is a promise from God that we will see such spiritual manifestations regularly if we follow the New Testament pattern. The Holy Spirit provides every believer with miracle power. The question is, what are we going to do with it? Power that is not recognized is power that is not released, and power that is not released is power that is not realized. If you want to see a miracle in your life, especially a miracle operating through you, you must place a claim on heaven!

APPLYING PRINCIPLES OF THE MIRACULOUS

THINKING IT OVER

1. Consider these "Miracle Insights" questions from page 26 of *School of the Miraculous*:

   + Why don't some Christians believe in miracles today?

   + What does the Greek word *dunamis* have to do with the miraculous? What is the Bible referring to when it mentions *dunamis* power?

   + What is the correlation between the Holy Spirit and miracles?

   + What does it mean to take a R-I-S-K in the kingdom of God?

2. Does your agenda for miracles match God's agenda for them?

ACTING ON IT

1. Have you received the baptism in the Holy Spirit? If not, pray the prayer found on page 23 of *School of the Miraculous* with expectancy.

2. Refer again to the acronym R-I-S-K. Think about how you can apply each action step to your faith in a practical way.

PRAYING ABOUT IT

Father, in the name of Your Son Jesus Christ, I thank You for Your presence and power in my life. I know that miracles are from You, and I desire to live a supernatural life. By faith, I receive and release Your *dunamis* power, the power to perform miracles! I recognize that the Holy Spirit is the source of supernatural power for the believer; therefore, I receive anew the infilling of the Holy Spirit. As I yield to Your Spirit, Your miracle power flows through every fiber of my being. I will never be the same again! In Jesus's name, amen!

MIRACLE TESTIMONY

A MIRACULOUS HEALING

A young girl in our church heard our teaching on miracles, signs, and wonders, and began to put it into practice. Even though she did not come from a Christian background, God began to do a work in her as she learned to yield to the Holy Spirit. One day, she was talking with her grandmother, who had been dealing with a chronic health condition for many years, and she began to release her faith for miracles, declaring her grandmother's healing in Jesus's name. Her grandmother was miraculously healed. This healing did not come through a tel-evangelist or prominent Christian minister, but through a ten-year-old child! Every believer can operate in the miraculous power of God.

ASK GOD TO GUIDE YOU IN PRAYING FOR SOMEONE WHO NEEDS HEALING.

CHAPTER 2

HEAVEN INVADING EARTH

CHAPTER THEME

The kingdom of God is His kingship, authority, influence, and government in the entire universe. When Jesus walked the earth, He proclaimed God's kingdom and released miracles everywhere He went. As a result of His ministry, the sick were healed, lepers were cleansed, the blind received sight, the deaf were enabled to hear, and people experienced a tangible touch from God. Likewise, as God's ambassadors, we have been charged with the responsibility of advancing His kingdom on earth, in all spheres of influence.

QUESTIONS FOR REFLECTION

+ When you think of the word *kingdom*, what comes to your mind?
+ What is the nature of the kingdom of God?
+ How does the kingdom of God compare to earthly kingdoms?

EXPLORING PRINCIPLES AND PURPOSES

1. The word kingdom literally means "_____."
   (p. 29)

2. List the two ways in which a kingdom typically expands. (p. 29)

    _____

    _____

3. When a kingdom conquers another kingdom or territory, it establishes its

    _____ and _____ over that territory. (p. 30)

4. Colonization is defined as "the action or process of _____ _____

    and _____ _____ _____ the indigenous people of

    an area." (p. 30)

5. The kingdom of God is His _____, _____,

    _____, and _____ in the entire universe, especially in

    the earth. (p. 30)

6. What is the kingdom of God characterized by? (p. 30)

    _____

    _____

    _____

7. Define the following terms: (p. 30)

    righteousness:

    _____

    _____

    _____

    peace:

    _____

    _____

    _____

joy:

_____

_____

_____

8. An essential distinction between the kingdom of God and earthly kingdoms is that the territory of God's kingdom on earth was _____ by the enemy, _____, whose sole intent is *"to steal, and to kill, and to destroy"* (John 10:10) this world, including human beings. (p. 30)

9. God's kingdom continually moves to _____ this lost territory and _____ a rule of love, peace, and joy on the earth. (p. 30)

10. The purpose of heaven is to _____ the earth. (p. 31)

11. We are _____ of the eternal King, _____ with the spiritual authority to _____ heaven into the earth. (p. 31)

12. Explain why the use of the expression *"in earth,"* rather than "on earth," in Matthew 6:10 is significant. (p. 31)

_____

_____

_____

13. Until heaven manifests in _____, it cannot manifest on _____. (p. 31)

14. How do we experience the demonstration of the kingdom? (p. 31)

_____

_____

_____

15. Miracles, signs, and wonders are the evidentiary _____ that heaven can and must invade our world. (p. 31)

16. What has every single believer been called and commissioned to do? (p. 32)

_____

_____

_____

_____

17. We must make ourselves _____ to God in obedient submission to His Word. (p. 33)

18. Willingness refers to our _____ and _____ to cooperate with God and His Word. (p. 33)

19. When we surrender to God, what are we are telling Him? (p. 33)

_____

_____

_____

20. We _____ to God's lordship, and then we become _____ of His delivering power. (p. 33)

CONCLUSION

As we yield to the kingdom of God *in* us, we begin to see the manifestation of the kingdom *through* us. We experience the demonstration of the kingdom by submitting to the government of God in our lives. As a result, the Holy Spirit colonizes the earth around us through His presence and power. This is the real purpose of miracles. The power of God is not meant to impress us or gratify our religious sentiments but to show the world that God is indeed King and His kingdom reigns over all the earth.

If you want to advance the kingdom of God, you must yield to the lordship of Jesus Christ daily. Remember, He is the sovereign King. When you submit to the agenda of the King, you will always see the manifestation of His kingdom.

APPLYING PRINCIPLES OF THE MIRACULOUS

THINKING IT OVER

1. Consider these "Miracle Insights" questions from page 36 of *School of the Miraculous*:

   o What does the Bible mean by the term "kingdom of God"?

   o When we receive God's Spirit, where is the kingdom of God located?

   o How do we release the kingdom of God in a practical way? What biblical examples do we have of releasing the kingdom?

   o What part does surrender play in our walking in miracles?

2. God rewards our willingness. Our willingness to yield to God is a major factor in seeing the manifestation of His power through us. How willing are you to obey the Word of God? How willing are you to be used by God? How willing are you to advance the kingdom on earth?

ACTING ON IT

1. Follow through with these "Practicum" exercises from page 37 of *School of the Miraculous*:

   o Read and meditate on Matthew 6:10 and 2 Corinthians 4:7, and then think about how God wants to establish His kingdom in you. Write down ways in which you may be trying to rely on your own abilities instead of God's strength to bring His kingdom to earth, and release those areas to him.

   o Begin to pray daily that God will show you specific ways in which He wants to use you to spread His kingdom on earth. Each day, pray, "Lord, I am available to You!"

   o Has God been directing you to reach out to someone in your sphere of influence? Step out in faith this week to contact that person, asking the Lord to use you to demonstrate His love and the power of His kingdom.

2. In what ways can you help bring righteousness, peace, and joy to your community?

PRAYING ABOUT IT

Father, I thank You for Your kingdom and majesty! As I yield to You in total surrender, I ask You to manifest Your kingdom in and through me. Forgive me for the areas in my life that I have not submitted to You. Forgive for me for exercising self-will. I fully confess my sin of disobedience and receive the truth of Your Word. I thank You that I am Your ambassador on earth, and that Your agenda is my agenda! I declare that when people see me, they will see Jesus and the culture of the kingdom of God. I embrace my ambassadorial assignment to advance Your kingdom on earth, within my circle of influence. I advance Your kingdom by operating in signs, wonders, and miracles. Thank You for all Your goodness! In Jesus's name, amen!

MIRACLE TESTIMONY

RESTORED FAITH, MARRIAGE, AND FINANCES

A lovely couple came to our ministry. The husband was unemployed and the wife was experiencing tremendous spiritual warfare, including health challenges. They were literally on the brink of divorce. The husband started to withdraw from the church community, but the wife continued to press in to God's Word. She kept coming to church and giving. Then the Lord began to speak to them both. As we continued to pray, God began to deliver the wife, and the couple's faith and marriage were restored. Their finances were also restored supernaturally. God is a God of miracles! If you will dare to contend for the supernatural, heaven will invade the earth.

ASK GOD TO DIRECT YOU TO PRAY AND PERSEVERE IN AN AREA OF YOUR LIFE WHERE YOU NEED TO CONTEND FOR HIS SUPERNATURAL POWER TO MANIFEST.

CHAPTER 3

DEVELOPING A SUPERNATURAL CULTURE

CHAPTER THEME

In the natural world, everything we see and experience is affected by and processed through the lens of our particular culture. As we grow in our understanding of the culture of God's kingdom (and spiritual matters in general), we will gain a God-centered outlook on the world. To walk in the supernatural, we must learn the culture of the kingdom and live in harmony with it.

QUESTIONS FOR REFLECTION

+ How would you define *culture*?

+ What are some of the major cultural characteristics of your community or nation?

EXPLORING PRINCIPLES AND PURPOSES

1. Philippians 3:20 says that *"our conversation* [manner of lifestyle, culture, citizenship] *is in heaven."* What does this mean for us as believers? (p. 41)

_____

_____

2. An integral feature of this heavenly culture is _____ power. (p. 41)

3. There are two main components to any culture: _____ and _____. (p. 41)

4. What is a good definition of *language?* (p. 41)

_____

_____

_____

_____

5. The primary language of the kingdom and its supernatural culture is _____. (p. 41)

6. If you want to see the miraculous, you need to _____ God's living words every day in faith. (p. 43)

7. God responds to expectation. When we doubt God, what are we telling Him? (p. 44)

_____

_____

_____

_____

8. Faith always speaks according to the _____ of God. (p. 44)

9. Faith doesn't _____ God do anything, but it does _____ us access to what He has already _____. (p. 44)

10. The _____ your faith, the _____ your access to the supernatural. (p. 45)

11. Define the word *custom*. (pp. 45–46)

_____

_____

_____

_____

12. One of the primary customs of the kingdom of God is a lifestyle of _____.
(p. 46)

13. Explain how we acquire holiness, and how we do *not* acquire it. (p. 46)

_____

_____

_____

_____

14. We walk in holiness by continually _____ to the leading and nature of the
Holy Spirit. (p. 46)

15. If we want to walk in power, we must make a deliberate and intentional decision to
_____ from wrongdoing and the appearance of evil. (pp. 46–47)

16. We must be intentional about separating ourselves from anything or anyone that would sap our
_____ _____ and _____. (p. 47)

17. What is another vital aspect of the customs of God's kingdom, and in what way is it like faith? (p. 49)

_____

_____

_____

18. What does "to honor" mean? (p. 49)

_____

_____

_____

_____

19. Define the Hebrew word for honor, *kabod*. (p. 49)

_____

_____

_____

_____

20. Honor is the _____ for the manifestation of God's
_____. Where there is no honor, there is no _____! (p. 51)

21. The anointing you _____ is the anointing you _____.
(p. 51)

CONCLUSION

Absorbing the culture of the supernatural is a key to releasing God's power. Two main components to any culture are language and customs. In the kingdom of God, the language of the supernatural is faith. Faith always speaks according to the Word of God. If we want to see the miraculous, we need to declare God's living words every day in faith. Faith action in the natural realm produces a response in the spiritual realm.

One of the primary customs of God's kingdom is a lifestyle of holiness. We walk in holiness by continually yielding to the leading and nature of the Holy Spirit. We must become mindful of our thoughts, attitudes, and conversations, as well as what we allow into our ear and eye gates. The more consecrated we are, the more spiritual power and authority we will walk in.

Another vital aspect of the customs of God's kingdom is the practice of showing honor. God will never manifest His glory in an atmosphere of dishonor. Faith and honor, combined with expectancy, create the environment for miracles.

APPLYING PRINCIPLES OF THE MIRACULOUS

THINKING IT OVER

1. Consider these "Miracle Insights" questions from page 54 of *School of the Miraculous*:
    - What does it mean to develop a supernatural culture?
    - What are the two major components to every culture? How important are language and culture in developing a supernatural lifestyle?
    - What is the "language of heaven"?
    - What is the relationship between honor and the miraculous?
2. On what have you been basing your holiness and righteousness before God? On the blood of Jesus, or on your own strength?

ACTING ON IT

1. Practice speaking the Word of God daily, including reciting particular Scriptures and reading the Bible aloud.
2. Be willing to conform your thinking to the Word of God consistently.
3. Demonstrate honor to a family member, church leader, or friend this week.

PRAYING ABOUT IT

Father, in the name of Jesus, I thank You for who You are and all that You have done in my life. I know that You are the righteous King and Your Kingdom is always advancing in the earth. Thank You for making me one of Your citizens through the blood of Jesus Christ and the power of Your Holy Spirit. I recognize that the language of heaven is faith and the customs of heaven are holiness and honor. Thank You for the revelation of biblical honor. As I release my faith in Your Word and walk in a culture of honor, I thank You that miracles will become more common in my life. I position myself right now to see the manifestation of Your supernatural power. In the precious name of Your Son, Jesus, I pray. Amen!

A MIRACLE OF SALVATION

One year, my wife and I hosted a birthday party for my daughter at our house. All of her friends and their parents were invited to come. One particularly close friend came to the party with her mother. As we began conversing with this parent, we discovered some very interesting things. She was an adherent of Rastafarianism, didn't believe in the God of the Bible, and was very cynical about Christianity and organized religion in general. She had been estranged from her husband and was dealing with substance abuse. I would love to say that we had a great conversation about the Lord that led to her salvation that night, but that's the exact opposite of what happened. We argued in my living room until the next morning. But before she left, I made a prophetic declaration over her life. I said that the God of the Bible would reveal Himself to her. Several months went by. Then, my wife received a phone call from her, inquiring about our church and the specific times of the services. To our surprise, this woman came to church the next Sunday with her children. She enjoyed the service, although she was not happy about my wife attempting to lead her children to Jesus.

But she came back again! And again! Eventually, she came to the altar for salvation. A few weeks later, her estranged husband moved back in with her and came to church and prayed the prayer of salvation. Her children were born again and filled with the Spirit of God. Both she and her husband were baptized. Their finances were turned around supernaturally, and they moved into a new home. Hallelujah! Make no mistake, the greatest miracle is the miracle of salvation.

ASK GOD TO LEAD YOU TO PRAY FOR THE MIRACLE OF SALVATION FOR A LOVED ONE OR FRIEND. THEN, ASK HIM TO GUIDE YOU IN YOUR INTERACTIONS WITH THIS PERSON SO THAT THE LIFE OF CHRIST WILL BE DEMONSTRATED IN YOU, AND GOD WILL BE GLORIFIED.

CHAPTER 4

KNOWING OUR IDENTITY

CHAPTER THEME

To walk consistently in God's miraculous power, we must know who we are in Him. Understanding our identity is one of the most important aspects of our spiritual life. We need to recognize that we are children of God and joint-heirs with Jesus. Everything we do in the kingdom depends on our comprehending our inheritance in Christ.

QUESTIONS FOR REFLECTION

+ What factors have most shaped your identity?
+ What is your perception of yourself as a Christian?

EXPLORING PRINCIPLES AND PURPOSES

1. Record Peter's response when Jesus asked His disciples, *"Whom do men say that I the Son of man am?"* (Matthew 16:13). (p. 57)

_____

_____

2. After Peter articulated the revelation of who Jesus was, he received the revelation of who he was. What did Jesus say about Peter's identity? (pp. 57, 59)

    _____

    _____

    _____

3. Identity is defined as "the _____ determining _____ or _____ a person or thing is." (p. 59)

4. We resemble God in our _____-_____! (p. 59)

5. You were not created to know God from afar. You were created to know Him _____ _____ and _____. (p. 59)

6. Adam's first encounter with God was face-to face, when God breathed into his nostrils the breath of life. What was one of God's purposes for this encounter? (p. 59)

    _____

    _____

    _____

    _____

7. We were meant to walk in the waking consciousness of who we are in _____. (p. 59)

8. Why does the devil want to keep people trapped in an identity crisis? (p. 60)

    _____

    _____

    _____

    _____

9. The Bible says that when we _____ Jesus as Savior and Lord, we are "_____ again." God puts His spiritual _____ inside us once more. We receive a new _____ identity. (p. 60)

10. We don't see true _____ until the One who created us puts His Spirit inside us and makes us a new creation. (p. 60)

11. Describe what the term "new creature" signifies. (p. 61)

_____

_____

_____

12. We have been born again of _____ seed by the same Spirit who raised Jesus from the dead. (p. 61)

13. We don't just "perform" the supernatural—we _____ supernatural. (p. 61)

14. God has called us to become His _____ and _____. (p. 63)

15. What are we able to do as part of our inheritance and identity in Christ? (p. 64)

_____

_____

_____

16. God, *El Shaddai*, is our all-sufficient _____ of everything we need. (p. 64)

17. We must become passionate about our _____ and _____ with the Father, not about the divine power itself, as important as it is for spreading God's kingdom on earth. (p. 64)

18. Because you are _____ Christ, His power and anointing are able to flow _____ you. (p. 65)

19. Jesus paid for your _____ of mind and heart when He died on the cross. Therefore, _____ is part of your inheritance. (p. 65)

20. What consciousness must we walk in for our lives, as modeled by Genesis? (p. 66)

_____

_____

_____

_____

21. Christ gave you His faith as your inheritance. Faith is _____ that God will do what He says He will do. Exercise God's faith so that it can grow in you. (p. 68)

22. Miracles work by faith, but faith works by the revelation of God's _____. (p. 68)

23. What is the means of all your provision? (p. 69)

_____

_____

_____

24. The enemy's strategy is for you to _____ what God has said, to cause you to think that He is capable of making a promise that He cannot keep. But God's Word is designed to bring us into a new _____, a new _____, of who we truly are. (p. 69)

25. Every area of bondage in a believer's life is connected to a _____ they have believed. The moment you _____ believing the lie and start believing the truth according to the Scriptures, the bondage is _____. (p. 69)

CONCLUSION

The promises, blessings, and benefits that we are ignorant of are the promises, blessings, and benefits that we are unable to receive. Satan tries to exploit our ignorance, using it as a weapon against us. God wants us to know what belongs to us so that we can believe Him for it!

When you were born again, you received an impartation of God's power and victory, and a new identity in Christ. The *"old man"* of sin and weakness has been done away with (see, for example, Romans 6:6) and a new creation has been born. Power and authority flow from identity. The more we realize and embrace who we are, the more the power of God will flow through us. Intimacy with God always produces miracles.

APPLYING PRINCIPLES OF THE MIRACULOUS

THINKING IT OVER

1. Consider these "Miracle Insights" questions from page 74 of *School of the Miraculous*:

    o What is the relationship between miracles and our identity as believers?

    o What does it mean to be "born again"? What took place spiritually when you were born again?

    o What does it mean to be born of "incorruptible seed"?

2. Has your perception of your identity changed since reading chapter 4 in *School of the Miraculous* and completing the corresponding questions in this study guide? If so, in what way(s)?

ACTING ON IT

1. Follow through with these "Practicum" exercises from pages 75–76 of *School of the Miraculous*:

    o Continue to renew your mind regarding your spiritual identity by committing these verses to memory:

    But as many as received Him, to them gave He power to become the sons of God, even to them that believe on His name. —John 1:12

    For as many as are led by the Spirit of God, they are the sons of God. —Romans 8:14

    If children, then heirs; heirs of God, and joint-heirs with Christ. —Romans 8:17

    Blessed be the God and Father of our Lord Jesus Christ, who has blessed us with all spiritual blessings in heavenly places in Christ. —Ephesians 1:3

o   Miracles manifest when we accept and receive who we are in Christ. Instead of "window shopping" in your relationship with God, confidently ask your heavenly Father to provide what you need and then rest in the knowledge of His care. Remember, your Father owns the whole store. Go in and receive!

2.   Based on the above memory verses and other biblical passages, make a list of key truths about who you are in Christ. Review your list each morning to remind yourself of your identity in God.

PRAYING ABOUT IT

Father, in the name of Jesus, I thank You for who You are and all that You have done in my life. I recognize that there is power in identity, and through Jesus, I have been given a new spirit and a new identity in You. I am not what I once was, but I have been cleansed from sin through the blood of Jesus and transformed by the power of the Holy Spirit. Thank You for causing me to grow in the revelation of who You are and the revelation of who I am in You. I was born for signs, wonders, and miracles, and I will walk in Your miraculous power daily. Because of the revelation of who I am in Christ, miracles and the supernatural are a common part of my life. I manifest the culture of heaven in the earth by walking in the flow of the Holy Spirit. Thank You for manifesting Your miraculous power through me. In Jesus's name, amen!

MIRACLE TESTIMONY

HEALED OF CEREBRAL PALSY

A woman who had been born with cerebral palsy came to me for prayer at a conference where I was preaching. I asked her if she wanted to be healed. Instead of laying hands on her and praying, I simply reminded her of who she was in Christ and told her that she could do all things through Christ who strengthened her. (See Philippians 4:13.) The more I made that declaration over her, the more her faith rose to the occasion. Suddenly, a woman who couldn't walk without someone supporting her was running around the entire sanctuary, shouting and giving glory to God. Hallelujah! The power of God is real, but its manifestation begins in our lives when we have a revelation of who God is and who we are in Him.

ASK GOD TO GIVE YOU A REVELATION OF WHO HE IS TO MEET A SPECIFIC NEED IN YOUR LIFE, WHETHER THAT NEED IS SICKNESS, A BROKEN RELATIONSHIP, FINANCIAL DIFFICULTY, OR ANYTHING ELSE.

CHAPTER 5

THE GLORY OF GOD

CHAPTER THEME

God is omnipresent, but He does not *manifest* Himself everywhere. The glory of God is the manifestation of His presence in a person or place. As believers, we are filled with God's glory. His miracle power dwells inside of us. The world is awaiting the release of what the Father has placed within each one of His children by His Spirit.

QUESTIONS FOR REFLECTION

- How would you describe God's glory?
- Have you ever experienced the presence of God in a palpable way?

EXPLORING PRINCIPLES AND PURPOSES

1. We cannot separate _____ God from _____ His presence. (p. 78)

2. In humanity's fallen state, God is _____ under normal circumstances and conditions. (p. 79)

3. We are new creations because God _____ us in Jesus! (p. 79)

4. God not only called us out of darkness into His _____, but He has also placed His light _____ us. (p. 80)

5. As a believer you are _____ with the glory of God. (p. 80)

6. Instead of thinking of miracles as something you need to achieve or accomplish, how should you regard them? (p. 80)

    _____

    _____

    _____

    _____

7. The glory of God is the _____ of heaven. It is a spiritual environment _____ by the senses. (p. 81)

8. Because the _____ of Jesus has cleansed us and the _____ _____ lives within us, we can continually abide in the presence of God. (p. 81)

9. Cultivating a _____ of _____ in God's presence is a key component to living in the miraculous. (p. 83)

10. Because of the life, death, and resurrection of Jesus Christ, there is a glory coming upon the _____ of God—not the building, but the _____—that has yet to be seen. (p. 83)

11. We are called to be glory-_____. (p. 85)

12. God has chosen us to _____ His presence and power to other people. (p. 85)

13. What will happen if we do not take our places as God's glory-carriers? (p. 85)

_____

_____

_____

14. God is raising up a generation of glory-carriers who will be so _____ to His presence that they will move whenever He _____ them to. (p. 86)

15. The world around us is _____ the release of what the Father has placed within each one of His children by His Spirit. (p. 86)

CONCLUSION

The King of Glory dwells in us by His Spirit! We actually carry the atmosphere of heaven. This is a deep truth. We must remember not to think of miracles as something we have to achieve or accomplish, but rather as something we release. As God's glory-carriers, we are to release His glory everywhere we go: homes, schools, churches, banks, places of work, and much more. Not only is this an amazing honor, but it is also a tremendous responsibility.

Certainly, God can manifest Himself to people without using human agencies, but He usually chooses to employ His followers for this purpose. In fact, almost every miracle in the Bible involves the employment of a human agency. We are God's agents, His ambassadors. So, the next time you go to work, school, or church, say, "The glorious presence of God dwells within me. I release this presence to flow out of me to those who need an encounter with God!"

APPLYING PRINCIPLES OF THE MIRACULOUS

THINKING IT OVER

1. Consider these "Miracle Insights" questions from page 88 of *School of the Miraculous*:
   o What is the Bible referring to when it talks about the "glory of God"?
   o What does it mean to be a glory-carrier?

- o What is the "greater glory" coming to the earth that is referenced in this chapter? What will it be characterized by?

- o What is the difference between how God's people experienced the glory of God in the Old Testament and how believers experienced His glory in the New Testament?

2. The more conscious and respectful we are of the presence of God, the more qualified we are to host the atmosphere of heaven. How can you be more conscious and respectful of God's presence in your life?

ACTING ON IT

1. Ask God to help you stop striving to make miracles happen and instead allow the Holy Spirit to release miracles through you.

2. Spend time in the presence of God daily, worshipping and praising Him, and retain a continuous awareness of His presence throughout the day. *"In Your presence is fullness of joy"* (Psalm 16:11).

3. Saturate your mind and spirit with God's Word so you can release His life-giving truth and power into your circumstances.

PRAYING ABOUT IT

Father, in the name of Jesus, I thank You for Your mighty power and presence working in and through my life. In 2 Corinthians 4:7, Your Word says, *"We have this treasure in earthen vessels, that the excellency of the power may be of God, and not of us."* Therefore, I declare that I am a glory-carrier! I hold Your glory within me through the Holy Spirit, and I am transformed by Your presence and power. I recognize that I am carrying the miracle that someone is waiting to experience. Father, please bring me into a greater consciousness of this truth. Awaken my spirit to the reality of Your presence in my life. By faith, I release the glory of God to those in my sphere of influence. I am not only a carrier of Your glorious presence, but I am also a benefactor of Your glory within me and upon me. I desire to be a part of the great awakening that You are releasing upon this generation. I make every part of my life available for Your glory. In the name of Jesus, amen!

MIRACLES OF BLESSING AND HEALING

J. reported, "I was listening to you on [Sid Roth's television program *It's Supernatural!*], speaking about getting into the presence of the Lord, and you said you start by singing the song "This Is the Air I Breathe." You prayed afterward for viewers, and as you were praying, I felt a heavy coolness being poured over my head. It was like oil being poured over me, but the coolness was like water. I gave God all the glory for the blessing I received.

Several years ago, my wife started to work out at the gym. She would get up every morning and make sure she got her workout in. Then, one day while she was at the gym, she severely injured her right arm and was in so much pain that she couldn't lift her arm to do anything. My wife thought it would be fine in a few days, but three days later, the pain was still excruciating. She made a trip to the emergency room but was told they couldn't treat her because she was pregnant. She went home, and I prayed over her from midnight until three in the morning. At three, I felt led to anoint her with oil and rebuke the injury. My wife said the pain decreased immediately. By noon, she barely felt any pain. When the orthopedic surgeon's office called to schedule her appointment, she told them, "I don't need you anymore! I am healed." Glory to God!

SEEK GOD'S HELP FOR A SPECIFIC PROBLEM IN YOUR LIFE BY SPENDING TIME IN HIS PRESENCE, WORSHIPPING HIM AND WAITING FOR THE MANIFESTATION OF HIS GUIDANCE AND PROVISION.

CHAPTER 6

THE POWER OF A RENEWED MIND

CHAPTER THEME

There is almost nothing more significant than the supernatural power of a transformed mind. The Bible tells us not to be conformed to the world but to take on a higher form by renewing our minds. You must undergo this transformation if you want to operate in miracles and live a supernatural lifestyle. Simply put, if you want to experience God on a greater level, you must change the way you think!

QUESTIONS FOR REFLECTION

- Do you expect to see miracles in your life and the lives of others every day?
- Do you anticipate the move of God everywhere you go?

EXPLORING PRINCIPLES AND PURPOSES

1. Romans 12:2 says, *"Be not conformed to this world: but be you transformed by the renewing of your mind, that you may prove what is that good, and acceptable, and perfect, will of God."* In this verse, what does the Greek word translated *"conformed"* mean? (p. 92)

_____

_____

2. In 1 John 2:15–16, what does the Bible mean by *"love not the world"*? In your answer, include what it *doesn't* mean by this term. (p. 92)

    _____

    _____

    _____

    _____

    _____

3. The *"lust of the flesh"* refers to a preoccupation with being gratified by what we can

    _____ or _____. (p. 93)

4. The *"lust of the eyes"* is an unwholesome desire to have the things that we _____. (p. 93)

5. The *"pride of life"* is basically _____. (p. 93)

6. The reality is, _____ has conditioned the human race to be preoccupied with our five human

    _____ —sight, hearing, smell, taste, and touch. (p. 93)

7. When we were born again, we were delivered from being _____ by

    our senses. (p. 93)

8. If we want to function supernaturally, in what ways must we be transformed?(p. 93)

    _____

    _____

    _____

9. In order to manifest the will and plan of God, we must embrace a _____

    _____-_____. (p. 93)

10. A spiritual outlook based on God's _____ and the work of His _____ is essential for releasing heaven on earth. (p. 94)

11. We already possess the _____ of Christ by virtue of the indwelling Holy Spirit, but we must learn to _____ to the mind of Christ daily. This requires us to actively _____ any thoughts that are not in alignment with the Word of God. (p. 94)

12. What happens every time we renew our mind? (p. 94)

_____

_____

_____

_____

13. The _____ of our souls has deliberately _____ many people and blinded them to the miraculous power and efficacy of the gospel of Jesus Christ. (p. 95)

14. We must develop a miracle _____. This is a spiritual framework that _____ us to walk in and release miracles *daily*. (p. 96)

15. Your paradigm affects your _____. (p. 96)

16. What are two reasons a person may be operating in unbelief? (p. 96)

_____

_____

17. God has given every believer a "_____ _____ _____"
(Romans 12:3). (p. 97)

18. In essence, doubting God's power is not about the absence of _____, but rather the presence of _____. (p. 98)

19. Every time we _____, _____, and _____ on the Word of God, we are renovating our mind and shifting our paradigm. (p. 99)

20. As believers, we are called to do the _____ that Jesus did—and even _____ _____, by His power within us. (p. 99)

CONCLUSION

If we are going to flow in the miraculous presence and power of God daily, we must believe that this life-style is available to us, and then release our faith to see, receive, and walk in it. "To believe" means not only to accept something as true, but also to act accordingly. As Christians, we are called to do the works that Jesus did—and even greater works. Do you really believe that? The proof is in the actions you take.

There is only one way to deal with the mental fortresses of doubt and unbelief: demolish them with the Word of God by faith! Our responsibility is to believe the Word of God, and God's responsibility is to manifest His power. If you will do the believing, He will do the manifesting.

APPLYING PRINCIPLES OF THE MIRACULOUS

THINKING IT OVER

1. Consider these "Miracle Insights" questions from page 103 of *School of the Miraculous*:
   o What does the Bible mean when it says, *"Be you transformed by the renewing of your mind"* (Romans 12:2)?
   o How can we be sure that every believer has faith?
   o What is the difference between *faith* and *believe*?
   o What is meant by the term "miracle paradigm"? How do we develop a miracle paradigm?

2. In what ways might you be "loving the world" in the sense described in this chapter? How can you renew your mind in these areas?

ACTING ON IT

1. Follow through with these "Practicum" exercises from page 104 of *School of the Miraculous*:
   o The renewal of our minds is the catalyst for supernatural transformation in our lives. Our thoughts, past experiences, and circumstances can create a negative mental fortress that

keeps us from the life God intends for us. Begin to develop a miracle paradigm by writing down areas in your life where you are operating in unbelief about seeing God move in the miraculous. Then, next to them, list corresponding Scripture passages that will renew your mind in those areas. Focus on these Scripture passages for an entire month, asking God to change your mind-set.

o   As you go about your day, whenever you have a thought or a process of reasoning that is opposed to the Word of God, stop and consider what you are thinking. Then, actively bring that thought into captivity to the obedience of Christ. (See 2 Corinthians 10:4–5.)

o   Action activates miracles. Remember this promise from Jesus: *"He that believes on Me, the works that I do shall he do also; and greater works than these shall he do; because I go to My Father"* (John 14:12). We have learned that faith is like currency, while believing is like credit. What person or circumstance will you pray for today, making a conscious decision to believe the Word of God rather than allow doubt and uncertainty to take over? Begin a journal to track your prayers for God's intervention, as well as His answers and miraculous manifestations.

2.   We can never base our theology solely on our personal experiences. Yet the more we grow spiritually, our personal experiences should be a reflection of sound theology. As you step out in faith, note the ways in which your personal experiences come into alignment with God's Word.

PRAYING ABOUT IT

Father, in the name of Jesus, I thank You for Your presence and miraculous power in my life. Your Word commands us to be transformed by the renewing of our mind. Therefore, I declare that my mind is renewed by the Word of God. I possess the mind of Christ. I think differently! Nothing is impossible to me because I am a believer and not a doubter! As I renew my mind through Your Word, strongholds of fear and unbelief are demolished by the power of Your Spirit. I believe in miracles! I will manifest the supernatural power of God in my life. I refuse to be a slave to fear, doubt, cowardice, or timidity. I press into miraculous breakthroughs by the persistent practice of believing Your Word and doing what it says, no matter what! Thank You, Father, for the promises of Your Word in my life. In Jesus's name, amen!

HEALED AFTER A STROKE

I related a testimony in my book *Invading the Heavens* that I think is a perfect illustration of how action activates miracles. I was in a meeting in which I prayed for a woman who had just experienced a stroke, causing her to lose the use of her right arm and her ability to speak. Because I was a man of great faith and power, I called her forward and declared that she was healed. Guess what happened after I prayed for her? Absolutely nothing! This was actually quite embarrassing for me, because I was focusing on myself instead of the Lord. In that moment, I realized that God wanted me to take my eyes off of myself and put my faith and confidence in Him. So, I continued to press in to the miracle.

All of a sudden, another level of faith rose up inside me. I told the woman to take the microphone that I was holding. The woman's friend told me that she couldn't grab the microphone because she was unable to use her arm due to the stroke. But God gave me boldness, so I insisted that the woman grab the microphone from my hand. Her friend actually became angry with me at that point, but I still insisted. As I continued to believe and press in to the miracle, something shifted in the spiritual atmosphere. The woman's faith began to rise up! Suddenly, she snatched the microphone from my hand and shouted, "JESUS!" Remember, she had not been able to speak since her stroke. Glory to God! The power of God touched this woman, and she was healed supernaturally! What would have happened if I had settled for the fact that nothing occurred the first time I prayed?

HAVE YOU GIVEN UP ON A MIRACLE AFTER HAVING PRAYED FOR IT ONE TIME OR FOR A SHORT PERIOD? ASK THE HOLY SPIRIT TO GUIDE YOU IN HOW TO PRAY AND FOLLOW HIS LEADING. TAKE THE FOCUS OFF YOURSELF AND PUT YOUR FAITH AND CONFIDENCE IN GOD.

CHAPTER 7

THE AUTHORITY OF PROCLAMATION

CHAPTER THEME

Every born-again believer has spiritual legislative authority in the kingdom of God. We are God's kings and priests (see Revelation 1:6; 5:10), and when we make a declaration in line with His will, spiritually speaking, it becomes "law." What you say has a tangible effect on the atmosphere around you. Speaking God's Word creates an atmosphere for miracles.

QUESTIONS FOR REFLECTION

+ How much consideration do you give to the words that you speak?

+ When have you seen a clear correlation between words you spoke and a result or consequence in your life or in someone else's life?

EXPLORING PRINCIPLES AND PURPOSES

1. What are two definitions of *proclamation?* (p. 105)

_____

_____

2. When our _____ are aligned with the _____ of God, they have "legal" authority in the spiritual realm. (p. 106)

3. As we join together with God and His Word, whatever we bind on earth is bound in heaven (_____ _____) and whatever is loosed on earth is loosed in heaven (_____ _____). (p. 106)

4. Speaking _____ words over people and situations can have an _____ effect on them. (p. 107)

5. The spiritual realm is a _____ reality than the natural realm. (p. 107)

6. God is a spiritual Being who governs by what He says. As human beings made in His image and likeness, what were we created to do? (p. 109)

_____

_____

_____

7. Your _____ indeed shape your _____. (p. 109)

8. What does it mean that death and life are in the "hand" of your tongue? (p. 110)

_____

_____

_____

_____

_____

9. We must be careful what we give _____ to by what we say or proclaim. (p. 110)

10. As you begin to change what you say, it is not about speaking some "magic words," but it is about consistently speaking _____-_____ words. (p. 111)

11. To experience God's power, we must make a daily habit of _____ the Word of God and making _____ of faith. (p. 112)

12. When you learn to live in a state of _____, constantly anticipating that God will move, you will consistently live in the miraculous. (p. 112)

13. _____ postures our heart in a state of expectancy. (p. 112)

14. In the spiritual realm, change begins with what we _____ and what we _____. (p. 113)

15. Every time we make a _____ by faith, in _____ with the Word, we are setting spiritual forces into motion that will ultimately manifest in our lives. (p. 113)

CONCLUSION

Operating in the supernatural power of God requires an understanding of the power of proclamation. Our words can either build or destroy. As we have learned, our words carry legal authority in the realm of the Spirit. This means that our words give license to matters and situations in our lives. We must be careful what we give license to by what we say or proclaim.

If you want your life to change, stop complaining and start proclaiming! Keep speaking God's Word until you see the manifestation. Miracles don't just happen for those who need them, but for those who expect them. The spirit of expectancy is indeed the catalyst for miracles. Every time you proclaim the Word of God in faith, you conform your world to God's Word. The more you proclaim, the more your life will reflect heaven.

THINKING IT OVER

1. Consider these "Miracle Insights" questions from page 116 of *School of the Miraculous*:

   o What is unique about proclaiming compared with any other form of speaking?

   o What are the spiritual implications of Matthew 18:18: *"Verily I say to you, Whatsoever you shall bind on earth shall be bound in heaven: and whatsoever you shall loose on earth shall be loosed in heaven"*?

   o Why isn't it usually enough to make a declaration once?

2. Consider the effect of your words on the spiritual atmosphere around you. How can you be more deliberate about speaking God's Word?

ACTING ON IT

1. For several days this week, take inventory of your words by jotting down recurring thoughts and statements. Then, next to each thought or statement, write down whether it aligns with God's Word or runs counter to it. For the thoughts and statements that run counter to the Word, write down verses that will help bring your words into alignment with God's nature and ways.

2. Begin to make the following declarations, which are based on Deuteronomy 28:13 and 2 Timothy 2:21:

   I am the head and not the tail.

   I am above only and not beneath.

   I am blessed in every area of my life.

   I am a vessel of honor, fit for God's use.

   I am full of supernatural power and grace.

   I am a vessel of the miraculous.

PRAYING ABOUT IT

Father, in the name of Jesus, I thank You for who You are and all that You continue to do in my life. Your Word declares that You created the universe with Your words. I recognize the profound power of Your words, including the supernatural power of proclaiming Your Word from my mouth daily. I recognize that speaking Your Word can shift the atmosphere and release miracles. Therefore, through the power of proclaiming, I release Your miracle power right now. People are healed when I speak Your Word. Chains are broken when I speak Your Word. Your glory is revealed when I speak Your Word. Thank You for teaching me how to guard the words of my mouth. I know that miracles will be my new normal, every day of my life. In the name of Jesus, amen!

MIRACLE TESTIMONY

MIRACULOUS FINANCIAL FAVOR

In obedience to God, my wife and I sowed into others' lives and paid people's rents and mortgages, and within a month, God blessed us with supernatural provision and a new car. Even the car salesman said he had never seen anyone receive such favor. The miracle of favor continues to overwhelm our ministry. As we have sown into good ground, we have seen a supernatural harvest time and time again.

Sister C. wrote to us, "We searched high and low for the owner of a rental home who would accept our application to rent. We tried over four applications, but no one would say yes because our circumstances are a little untraditional. We sowed a seed in church last Sunday and arrived home to a yes application. We are moving in to our new home today."

MIRACULOUS PROVISION FOR DEBT

Several years ago, the Lord impressed upon my heart to take my congregation through a series of prophetic prayers regarding debt cancellation. I told them that within thirty days, many would experience a supernatural cancellation of their debt. One such individual was a young lady who received a phone call from her parents, who informed her that an account had been opened in her name when she was a baby and that this account had matured and was available for making withdrawals. The next day, she went to the bank and made a withdrawal from the account that covered all of her debts. I believe God is releasing financial miracles all over the earth today! Are you ready to receive a financial miracle? Are you ready for your debts to be canceled supernaturally?

IF YOU HAVE A FINANCIAL NEED, FOLLOW GOOD MONETARY PRACTICES. OBEY WHAT THE BIBLE SAYS ABOUT FINANCES AND DEVELOP A GIVING SPIRIT AS YOU STEADFASTLY PROCLAIM GOD'S PROMISES OF PROVISION.

CHAPTER 8

RELEASING THE SUPERNATURAL

CHAPTER THEME

"The anointing" is another significant facet of living a supernatural lifestyle. We must fully realize this fact: everything Jesus did while He was on the earth, He did as the Son of Man, anointed by the Holy Spirit. He did not operate as deity, even though He was fully God as well as fully man. The good news is that, as believers, we have the same anointing residing within and resting upon us! When the Bible speaks of the anointing, it is talking about the dynamic, yoke-destroying, burden-removing, supernatural power of God that operates within every believer.

QUESTIONS FOR REFLECTION

+ What do you think of when you hear the term "the anointing"?
+ Do you believe you are anointed by God to do His work? Why or why not?

EXPLORING PRINCIPLES AND PURPOSES

1. The Anointed One (Jesus) and His anointing truly _____ in us. (p. 120)

2. The term "Christ" is not Jesus's last name, but rather means "_____." He is the Source from which all heavenly anointing flows. (p. 120)

3. The Scriptures often depict the anointing as _____. (p. 120)

4. Define the Greek word translated *"anointing"* in 1 John 2:27: (p. 120)

_____

_____

_____

5. In biblical times, fragrant oil would be poured on the priests' heads, signifying the _____ _____ _____ upon their lives. You recognized the priests not only by their garments, but also by their _____ of oil. (pp. 120–21)

6. Because we are kings and priests to God through Jesus Christ, we are anointed and carry the aroma of _____. (p. 121)

7. The "oil," or anointing, destroys _____ and removes _____, not only in our lives, but also in the lives of the people with whom we come into contact. (p. 121)

8. What are the main characteristics of God's anointing? (p. 121)

_____

_____

_____

9. The anointing is tangible in that it can often be _____ or sensed. (p. 121)

10. The anointing is transferable in that it can be _____ from one person or thing to another person or thing. (p. 122)

11. The key is to activate and release the anointing through _____ and _____. (p. 123)

12. What will happen when you obey the assignment God has placed upon your life? (p. 123)

_____

_____

_____

13. You activate the anointing by _____ _____ God's Word. (p. 125)

14. Connecting to an anointing on someone else's life (through books, teachings, and relationships) can _____ the anointing on your life. (p. 127)

15. The anointing is _____, not taught. (p. 127)

16. In the natural world, *surrender* means "to stop resisting…an enemy or opponent and submit to their authority." In what context is *surrender* used in *School of the Miraculous?* (p. 128)

_____

_____

_____

17. When it comes to the anointing of the Holy Spirit, we must learn how to _____ to Him, submitting to His power and authority. (p. 128)

CONCLUSION

If the Spirit of God lives in you, then you are extraordinary. You are anointed! The more you understand the anointing, the more you will begin to operate in it. The key is to activate and release that anointing through faith and obedience. Jesus is the Source from which all heavenly anointing flows. When we yield to Him, we yield to His anointing—the power of God working in and through us. Spiritual power is increased through our surrender and submission to God.

One of the keys to receiving, increasing, and walking in the anointing is a connection with another believer. Elisha had to stay connected with Elijah if he wanted to receive a double portion of the anointing his mentor had. This biblical principle of connection is a challenge for us in the transient and individualistic Western culture of our day. Many people don't stay connected to anyone or anything long enough to receive what God has for them.

If you want to operate in the anointing and live in the miraculous, you must remain "connected" and "plugged in" to the Power Source, the Holy Spirit. Meditate on God's Word, pray, yield to the Holy Spirit's leading, and stay connected to other believers in a life-giving community.

APPLYING PRINCIPLES OF THE MIRACULOUS

THINKING IT OVER

1. Consider these "Miracle Insights" questions from page 129 of *School of the Miraculous*:
   o What is the biblical definition of "the anointing"?
   o Who would you consider anointed? What makes them anointed?
   o Can the anointing increase in a person's life? If so, how?
   o With regard to the "mystery of Elijah's mantle," what are the two spiritual laws that cause a person to increase in the anointing?

2. How have you seen God's anointing manifested in and through you to minister to others?

ACTING ON IT

1. Follow through with these "Practicum" exercises from page 131 of *School of the Miraculous*:
   o Read the following portions of Scripture, keeping in mind that whenever Jesus acted on earth, He did not operate as deity but as the Son of Man, anointed by the Holy Spirit: Matthew 14:13–21; Luke 8. Then, remind yourself that you have the same anointing residing within and resting upon you!
   o Perhaps you don't "feel" anointed. What does the Word of God say about this in 1 John 2:27? How will you allow God's truth to change your perspective on your anointing?
   o You have been anointed by God to destroy oppressive yokes and remove burdens. Begin to live in the power of the Anointed One and His anointing. Ask God to use you as a vessel to transfer His supernatural power to people and situations in need of a miracle. Begin by sharing your faith with someone else and allowing God to work from there.

2. The anointing is caught, not taught. What steps can you take to get closer to the anointing that you want to receive? Who in your life has an anointing they can impart to increase your anointing?

PRAYING ABOUT IT

Father, in the name of Jesus of Nazareth, I thank You for who You are and Your precious anointing. Your Word says that the anointing destroys the yoke and removes heavy burdens. I recognize that the anointing I have received from You abides in me and is truth. I also recognize that the Holy Spirit within me is the Power Source of any and all anointing. I declare that Your power and presence in my life increase because I surrender to You in obedient submission to Your Word. As I yield to Your Word and Spirit, I release the supernatural in my life. I am anointed to operate in signs, wonders, and miracles. As I remain connected to the Anointed One and His anointing, chains are broken off of my life and the lives of those around me. I receive a supernatural impartation from You to see miracles in my life daily. I am anointed to see a move of God in my life. In Jesus's name, amen!

MIRACLE TESTIMONY

AN INCREASE IN ANOINTING

One day, a young lady in my church came to me and said, "Pastor, I want a double portion of the anointing that's on your life." As new covenant believers, with the Holy Spirit living within us, I don't believe we need to ask anyone for a double portion, but I do believe that God desires that we all increase in the anointing daily. So, I prayed for her that God would give her the desire of her heart. When I prayed for this precious woman, she fell under the power of God and was filled with the Holy Spirit. From that day forward, she began to walk in signs and wonders. Every time I saw her, she had another testimony of a miracle that had recently taken place. Hallelujah! She was willing to humble herself and submit to my spiritual authority. Some people would be too proud to make such a request.

ASK GOD DAILY TO FILL YOU ANEW WITH THE HOLY SPIRIT AND TO RELEASE THE ANOINTING THAT IS WITHIN YOU TO MEET THE NEEDS OF PEOPLE AROUND YOU.

CHAPTER 9

BREAKING THE STRONGHOLD OF FEAR

CHAPTER THEME

If you are going to live a miraculous life, you must conquer fear. Fear manifests in our lives in many ways and hinders us from becoming all that God wants us to be.

Fear is motivated by what we think, see, or hear in the physical world. Faith is motivated by what God says and does! God can overcome all our fears, to His glory. Two thousand years ago, Jesus triumphed over fear on the cross, and we must appropriate His victory today in our lives.

QUESTIONS FOR REFLECTION

+   What fears do you especially struggle with?
+   How has the Word of God helped you to overcome fear?

EXPLORING PRINCIPLES AND PURPOSES

1.   List some ways in which fear manifests in our lives: (p. 134)

    _____

    _____

2. Satan's agenda is to use fear to _____ and control us,

   _____ our perception and thinking processes, and keep us

   _____ in his deceptions so we cannot live in the power of God. (p. 134)

3. First John 4:18 says, *"There is no fear in* _____*."* (p. 134)

4. We cannot be in _____ and in _____ at the same time because faith works

   by love. (See Galatians 5:6.) (p. 135)

5. When we fear, we accept "evidence" that appears real but is _____. (p. 135)

6. There are natural fears, based on genuine threats. However, even then, God's love and faith can

   replace our fear with trust in His _____, _____, and

   _____. (p. 135)

7. Which two types of fears must we recognize the difference between? (p. 135)

   _____

   _____

8. It is important to note that _____ in a state of fear is

   unnatural. We should never continue in any negative state for a prolonged period of time

   because it can have a damaging effect on us _____,

   _____, _____, or

   _____. (p. 135)

9. It is nearly impossible to exercise spiritual _____ while

   simultaneously operating in fear. (p. 136)

10. Define the word *stronghold* in both a natural and spiritual sense. (p. 136)

    _____

    _____

_____

_____

11. Explain why the devil uses spiritual strongholds like fear in people's lives. (p. 136)

_____

_____

_____

12. Satan's strongholds cannot stand up against the _____ of God's Word and the _____ of His Spirit. (p. 137)

13. The enemy of our soul uses _____ _____ and _____ _____ to erect strongholds in our spiritual life. (p. 137)

14. Fear is a _____, and like all spirits, it must bow to the authority of the name of Jesus! (p. 138)

15. Just as _____ facilitates the miraculous power of God, _____ facilitates the destructive power of the enemy. (p. 138)

16. Every area of bondage in a believer's life is connected to a _____ they have believed— about God, themselves, or their circumstances. (p. 138)

17. The devil wants to keep many people trapped in fear because if they continue to believe lies about themselves or others, they will remain in a place of _____ or become further _____ in their faith. (p. 138)

18. Jesus calls us beyond the place of fear into the place of faith, where we are _____ to live supernaturally. (p. 138)

19. What two elements, which are the opposite of fearfulness, does walking in the supernatural power of God require? (p. 141)

_____

_____

20. Every time we take a step of faith, we are positioned to experience a greater _____ of God's power. (p. 141)

21. If you will take your eyes off of yourself and place them on your _____, things will drastically shift in your life. (p. 141)

CONCLUSION

The nature of our born-again spirit is faith and power, not fear and paralysis. We were not created for fear and worry.

The enemy of our soul uses deceitful arguments and false images to erect strongholds in our spiritual life. But God is raising up a generation of people who will break the stronghold of fear and insecurity and will move into the sphere of power and influence that God has ordained for them.

To operate in signs and wonders consistently and effectively, you need to rid yourself of an attitude of fear! You must be confident of God's power within you. We cannot be in fear and faith at the same time because faith works by love. Faith is the necessary ingredient to overcoming the power of fear. Faith leads to action, and action activates miracles!

APPLYING PRINCIPLES OF THE MIRACULOUS

THINKING IT OVER

1. Consider these "Miracle Insights" questions from page 143 of *School of the Miraculous*:
   o What role does fear potentially play in hindering the miraculous power of God from working in your life?
   o What is the difference between rational and irrational fears?
   o Name three of the major fears that Christians have regarding the idea of God operating through them.

o How do we overcome fear in our life?

2. Identify one lie that Satan has used to keep you trapped in bondage to fear. How can you counter that lie with the Word of God?

ACTING ON IT

1. Develop a plan for confronting your fears according to the principles in this chapter. How can faith help you overcome these fears? Remember, once you confront a fear, it loses its power.

2. Do a work for the kingdom of God that you have never done before. Step out in a tangible and measurable way today. Don't worry about your past, your problems, or your perceived limitations. Just tell God, "I am available to You! Do a miracle through my life in the power of Your Spirit."

PRAYING ABOUT IT

Father, in the name of Jesus, I thank You that You are love, and that You are the God of love. There is no fear in love because perfect love casts out fear. Thank You for the Spirit of faith and confidence in Your Word. I refuse to submit to the power of fear! Through faith in Your Word, I demolish the stronghold of fear in my life and in the lives of others. I take authority over the spirit of fear. I have not received a spirit of fear but a spirit of power, love, and a sound mind. Therefore, I will never be afraid to take a risk when I know You are leading me to step out in faith. I live a life of fearless faith and boldness. Thank You for removing the residue of fear, guilt, and shame from my life. Through the authority of Your Word, I make fear bow. Thank You for delivering me from the spirit of timidity, cowardice, and self-consciousness. In the name of Jesus, amen!

MIRACLE TESTIMONY

A MIRACLE OF CONCEPTION

A couple in our church had not been able to conceive a child for many years. After much prayer and no results, they had become quite frustrated with the situation. They came to us and asked us to pray for "the fruit of the womb." Within several months, the wife conceived, and she gave birth to a beautiful, healthy baby. Glory to God!

If you know my wife and me, you know that we are no strangers to childbirth. (We now have five children.) After our first two children, I think we became experts. However, God began to show us a more excellent way when it came to faith and miracles. This was especially relevant to giving birth to children. Trust me, I am well aware that my wife is the one who gave birth to all of our children, and not me, as the nurse would so eloquently remind me. But God was shifting us! My wife got hold of a teaching on supernatural childbirth. She learned that she didn't have to settle for what family members or programs on television say childbirth has to be. We realized that pain in childbearing was a function of the curse. My wife made up her mind that it was not God's will for her to suffer in the delivery room. She declared that the curse upon Eve was not applicable to her, and she has experienced supernatural deliveries with little to no pain. In fact, my son came out so fast that the midwife had to catch him by the leg! If I hadn't been in the delivery room, I probably wouldn't have believed it myself. After the delivery, the midwife and staff told us that it was the most amazing birth they had ever seen. Hallelujah!

PRAY FOR GOD'S SUPERNATURAL INTERVENTION IN THE LIVES OF WOMEN WHO ARE INFERTILE, HAVING DIFFICULTIES IN THEIR PREGNANCIES, OR EXPERIENCING PAIN IN CHILDBIRTH.

CHAPTER 10

THE SPIRIT OF AWAKENING

CHAPTER THEME

For a long time, the church of the Lord Jesus Christ has been asleep. Yes, we have had spurts of revival and breakthrough over the years, but these jolts of miraculous power were intended to do more than excite us; they were meant to awaken the church so that we could move in the divine purpose of God.

It was always God's design that the Holy Spirit would flow from the believer's innermost being. We were never meant to be like a shallow lake or stagnant pond, but a living river. Just as the might and power of natural waves and storm surges are capable of flooding entire cities, God desires to flood cities and nations with the culture of His kingdom—a culture of awakening and reformation.

QUESTIONS FOR REFLECTION

+ Would you say you are more self-conscious or God-conscious? Why?

+ How would you define the words *revival* and *awakening?*

EXPLORING PRINCIPLES AND PURPOSES

1. The next great move of the God is coming from _____—within *us*! It's not coming down; it's coming _____! (p. 146)

2. Unfortunately, we have often built shrines around the _____ of revival rather than seeking the _____ who revives us. (p. 146)

3. It is good to remember, appreciate, and learn from past revivals, but the danger is in _____ there. (p. 146)

4. Revival was always meant to be a means to an end—the spiritual _____ of the church. (p. 147)

5. Define the word *awakening* from *Merriam-Webster's* dictionary: (p. 147)

   _____

   _____

6. What are we to come into an awareness of? (p. 147)

   _____

   _____

   _____

   _____

   _____

7. All human beings were meant to have _____ encounters with God and to be filled with Him! (p. 149)

8. We were designed to have _____ over the earth in the context of _____ with and _____ to God. (p. 149)

9. What must we understand, in a deep way, if we are going to see the power of God flow through us? (pp. 149, 151)

_____

_____

_____

10. In Genesis 3, we learn that Adam and Eve believed the lie of Satan and disobeyed God by eating the fruit of the Tree of Knowledge of Good and Evil. As a result, the entire human race became spiritually _____ from God—we lost the glory and intimacy with Him that we once had. This glory and relationship with God is what Jesus came to _____. Receiving and living in this restoration is the key to a supernatural life. (p. 151)

11. We must learn not to be discouraged by the negative opinions of others, particularly when those opinions are in _____ to the Word of God. (p. 153)

12. How is the term *God-consciousness* described in this chapter? (p. 153)

_____

_____

_____

_____

_____

13. How is *self-consciousness* described? (p. 155)

_____

_____

_____

_____

14. We can move from self-consciousness to God-consciousness by responding to the work of the Spirit in our life and experiencing a _____ _____. (p. 155)

15. Who is the key to bringing the life of God "on earth as it is in heaven"? (p. 156)

_____

_____

_____

_____

CONCLUSION

Nothing can take the place of a personal supernatural awakening. When we are impacted, on a personal level, with the reality of who Jesus is, our lives are profoundly transformed.

It all begins with the focus of your consciousness. Your consciousness determines your level of awareness, and your level of awareness determines your level of awakening. Are you self-conscious or God-conscious? The answer to this question will determine your capacity for the miraculous. The Holy Spirit is the key to bringing the life of God "on earth as it is in heaven" because He moves us from self-consciousness to God-consciousness.

APPLYING PRINCIPLES OF THE MIRACULOUS

THINKING IT OVER

1. Consider these "Miracle Insights" questions from page 158 of *School of the Miraculous*:
   o Is there a difference between revival and awakening? If so, what is the difference?
   o Where is the next great move of God going to come from?
   o What does the Scripture mean when it says that living water will flow out of our innermost being?
   o What is the difference between God-consciousness and self-consciousness?

2. Global revival starts with personal revival. The transformation of culture begins with the transformation of character. In what ways have you experienced personal revival and awakening?

ACTING ON IT

1. Follow through with these "Practicum" exercises from page 159 of *School of the Miraculous*:

   o If you tend to focus on your frailties and sin, meditate on God's Word and worship Him consistently each day so that you can remain continually aware of God's presence and provision for you.

   o Ask God to give you a personal supernatural awakening of the reality of who Jesus is and what He has done for you, so you can experience an infilling of the Holy Spirit and healing from the hurts, discouragements, and failings of the past. Remember that God is a God of new beginnings! Ask Him to move in supernatural ways in your life so you can testify of His miraculous kingdom power and minister that power to others.

   o Have you ever received negative comments from other people for having supernatural encounters with God or walking in the miraculous? If so, how did you react? Don't be discouraged about these negative experiences, but give them to God and keep moving forward in His kingdom purposes. Allow these Bible passages to encourage you: 2 Corinthians 1:3–7 and Philippians 4:4–8.

2. Pray for the awakening of the church so God's people can move in His divine purposes and spread the culture of His kingdom on earth.

PRAYING ABOUT IT

Father, in the name of Jesus, I thank You for Your *mighty power*! Thank You for the spirit of revelation in the knowledge of You. Thank You for awakening me out of spiritual slumber and bringing me into the consciousness of who You are and what You have given me in Christ. I declare that the spirit of slumber is broken off of me, my family, and my community, in the name of Jesus. Lord, just as Adam and Eve walked with You in the cool of the day, I desire intimate fellowship with You. Bring me into the reality of Your supernatural presence and power daily. Cleanse my life from anything that would hinder my fellowship with You. It is my desire to please You in every area of my life. Therefore, I receive the cleansing that comes from Your Word to make me a vessel of honor, sanctified and fit for the Master's use. I declare that awakening touches everyone around me. In the name of Jesus, amen!

SUPERNATURAL ENCOUNTERS

In the summer of 1996, I was a zealous young Christian, adamant about receiving everything God had for me. I asked God for the baptism in the Holy Spirit, and when I received the baptism, my life was radically transformed. I immediately began to have supernatural encounters with God. Some of these encounters were so significant that they permanently changed the way I saw my heavenly Father. He was more than just a distant deity whom I learned about in Bible study. He was real; He was substantial. *He loved me!*

The first types of supernatural encounters I experienced were prophetic utterances and words of knowledge. These communications from God are among the gifts of the Spirit that Paul writes about in 1 Corinthians 12. God began showing me information and insights about people (myself included) and about the church globally, and I would speak out prophetic words in church. It was amazing!

The second type of supernatural encounter I had was angelic visitations. That's right! I began sensing and seeing angels. I vividly remember a particular encounter in which I met an angel at a bus stop. I saw a man who looked very peculiar, in the sense that I could not place his ethnicity. He looked like all the tribes of the earth in one. This man asked me to tell him the time, and then he vanished into thin air! I looked everywhere and could not find him. I knew in my spirit that I had "entertained" an angelic being:

> *Be not forgetful to entertain strangers: for thereby some have entertained angels unawares.*
>
> —Hebrews 13:2

ASK GOD TO BAPTIZE YOU IN HIS HOLY SPIRIT AND FILL YOU WITH THE CONSCIOUSNESS OF HIS PRESENCE.

CHAPTER 11

EVERYDAY MIRACLES AND THE POWER OF PRAYER

CHAPTER THEME

The attitude of expectancy is the atmosphere for miracles. The more you develop an expectation for the miraculous, the more miracles you will see. You may ask, "Can I really walk in miracles daily?" A better question would be, "Do I really *want* to walk in miracles daily?" If you have a spirit of expectation every single day, you will see the manifestation of that anticipation.

QUESTIONS FOR REFLECTION

+ What is the purpose of prayer?

+ What miracle or other work has God recently done in your life?

EXPLORING PRINCIPLES AND PURPOSES

1. Expectation leads to _____. (p. 163)

2. Consistent _____ is the catalyst for a spirit of expectancy. (p. 163)

3. Prayer energizes our spiritual lives and postures us to _____ the things of the Spirit. (p. 163)

4. What happens the more we pray and increase our level of expectation? (p. 163)

_____

_____

_____

_____

5. _____ is an expectancy killer! It brings guilt, shame, and condemnation. (p. 164)

6. One of the most debilitating forces in the life of a believer is _____ and
_____. When Christians refuse to _____ those who
have hurt, disappointed, or wounded them, they open their lives to spiritual darkness. (p. 164)

7. Our faith works by love. Therefore, if we are offended, resentful, and bitter, what is the result?
(p. 165)

_____

_____

_____

_____

8. Within the pattern of the Lord's Prayer, we are admonished to ask for and _____
our daily bread. This request does not just refer to physical food, but also to the miraculous
_____ and _____ of God in our lives—*every single day.*
(pp. 165–66)

9. Prayer is like plugging into an electrical outlet. The stronger the connection, the greater the
_____ of power released. (p. 166)

10. The Scriptures are very clear that we are to pray without ceasing. What is the only way we can do this? (p. 167)

_____

_____

_____

_____

11. Every time we pray in _____, we build up our spirit in faith. Praying in tongues alone does not give us faith, but it _____ and builds the faith we already possess. (p. 169)

12. Prayer is one of the means through which we _____ our mind. Prayer cultivates the _____ _____ _____ within us. (p. 169)

13. We can train ourselves to develop a _____ perspective about the _____ circumstances in our lives. (p. 170)

14. Through what means was Jesus able to gain access to the heart, mind, and will of His heavenly Father so He could carry out God's purposes on earth? (p. 170)

_____

_____

_____

_____

15. As we begin to walk in miracles daily, we must keep in mind that receiving miracles is not a matter of human effort, but rather a byproduct of "the _____ of faith." The Bible says that "_faith comes by hearing, and hearing by the word of God_" (Romans 10:17). (p. 171)

16. Miracles are not random acts of God's sovereignty; instead, they are a part of our _____ in Christ. (p. 172)

CONCLUSION

Living in a continual state of expectation positions us to experience the miraculous. Consistent prayer is the catalyst for a spirit of expectancy. The Scriptures tell us, *"Pray without ceasing"* (1 Thessalonians 5:17). Prayer connects us to the spiritual realm, where miracles are born. The more we pray according to the will of God, the more we increase our expectations.

Praying in the Holy Spirit activates our spirits and causes us to be sensitive to the presence and power of God. Through prayer, we partner with heaven to see the purposes of God manifested. God desires to show His glory in the earth, but we must make this purpose our passionate daily pursuit. God will never encroach upon the human will. He invites us into kingdom realities, but we must exercise our faith and volition in order to walk in them.

APPLYING PRINCIPLES OF THE MIRACULOUS

THINKING IT OVER

1. Consider these "Miracle Insights" questions from page 175 of *School of the Miraculous*:
   o How do we develop an attitude of expectancy?
   o What are some things that can hinder our expectancy?
   o What role does prayer play in our walking in the miraculous consistently?
   o How is receiving miracles a byproduct of "the hearing of faith"?

2. To pray in the Spirit means to pray Spirit-directed prayers. Often, it means praying in a God-given language, a "tongue of men or of angels." (See 1 Corinthians 13:1.) Praying in tongues is a secret weapon in supernatural living. How often do you pray in tongues? Have you asked God to baptize you in the Holy Spirit and give you this gift?

ACTING ON IT

1. Everywhere you go, be looking for ways in which God is working. Decide to live in the anticipation that something miraculous will occur. Expect miracles today and every day.

2. Embrace a lifestyle of prayer and intercession, remembering that we develop an attitude of expectancy through prayer in harmony with God's Word.

3. You cannot walk in condemnation and expectancy at the same time. If there is anything in your life that is causing you guilt, shame, or condemnation before the Lord, lay it down at His feet right now. Acknowledge whatever it is, repent of it, and turn back to God in faith and expectancy.

4. We can train ourselves to develop a supernatural perspective about the natural circumstances in our lives. Make these declarations every day:

> I have the mind of Christ. Therefore, I see the world around me from a heavenly perspective. Natural limitations are not a hindrance for me.

> Today, I will hear the voice of the Holy Spirit, respond to His instruction, and release the power of God. Today, I will see miracles in my life and in the lives of those around me. I will partner with God to see the supernatural life of heaven become a reality on earth.

PRAYING ABOUT IT

Father, in the name of Jesus Christ, I thank You for Your miraculous power working in me. Today, I release my expectancy for miracles, signs, and wonders. I recognize that You want to do something supernatural through my life daily. I acknowledge the power of prayer, and by faith, I access spiritual realities that go beyond the limitations of my circumstances. Father, whatever You have promised me, and whatever You have spoken concerning my life, I receive it right now. I declare that I am a vessel You have raised up in this generation to release miracles. I declare that Your Spirit catapults me into new dimensions of the supernatural presence and power of God. I am anticipating great things happening in my life because You are omnipotent and omnibenevolent. In Jesus's name, amen!

MIRACLE TESTIMONY

MIRACLES OF PROVISION

At one point, the Lord began to speak to my wife and me about all-night prayer. This had been a part of the culture of our church for years, but I felt like God was calling us back to that level of devotion. We began to engage in all-night prayer. During one specific season of prayer, God sent miraculous provision. Businesses began to donate things to the church. In fact, one of the top companies in our area offered thousands of dollars of services for free. Hallelujah!

In another instance, during the youth service, our nine-year-old daughter declared that she saw a vision. In this vision, during prayer, God released everything we needed for the church, but a huge spider's web held it back. Then, in this vision, she saw the web destroyed by the power of God—and the blessings were released. A week later, we got a call informing us that a brand new office suite, furniture, appliances, and equipment worth over twenty thousand dollars were being donated to us! Glory to God!

ASK GOD TO DIRECT YOU AS YOU PRAY FOR HIS WILL TO BE DONE ON EARTH AS IT IS IN HEAVEN. TRUST HIM TO PROVIDE FOR ALL YOUR NEEDS.

CHAPTER 12

SPIRITUAL GIFTS AND THE MIRACULOUS

CHAPTER THEME

In order to walk in the miraculous daily, it is very important to understand the purpose and power of spiritual gifts. The more you learn about spiritual gifts, the more you will be able to operate in them consistently. In essence, spiritual gifts demonstrate to people that the Holy Spirit and the world to come are very real. The more intimate we are with the Holy Spirit, the more we will be able to operate in His gifts.

QUESTIONS FOR REFLECTION

- What does the term "spiritual gifts" refer to?

- Which spiritual gift are you most familiar with? Why?

EXPLORING PRINCIPLES AND PURPOSES

1. Spiritual gifts are special _____ of the Holy Spirit that He distributes through and for various people and environments, for the _____ of the body of Christ. (p. 179)

2. Name the nine spiritual gifts listed in 1 Corinthians 12: (p. 179)

_____

_____

_____

_____

_____

_____

_____

3. It is the same Spirit manifesting in _____ ways for the collective benefit of the body of Christ. (p. 181)

4. The apostle Paul encourages the church to _____ the way the Holy Spirit manifests through each believer, and never to be _____ or _____ based upon a particular gifting. (p. 181)

5. The Holy Spirit is the most _____ Person on earth, and one of His roles as our Helper is to endow us with supernatural function. (p. 183)

6. We have been empowered by the Spirit of God to be _____ of the resurrection of Jesus Christ. One of the ways in which we do this is through the exercise of spiritual gifts. (p. 183)

7. The word of wisdom is designed to instruct, exhort, and console the body of Christ. What is this gift a supernatural revelation of? (p. 183)

_____

_____

_____

8. Often, a word of knowledge is actually a _____ or an
_____ given to someone by the Holy Spirit. But what really makes it a
word of knowledge is when it is _____. (p. 184)

9. The purpose of a word of knowledge is to benefit the _____, not to gratify the
_____. (p. 184)

10. The gift of faith is a special endowment of the Holy Spirit to _____ God for
a specific manifestation or outcome. (p. 185)

11. Which other gift does the gift of faith often accompany? (p. 185)

_____

_____

_____

_____

12. Gifts of healing are supernatural manifestations of God's healing power through the Holy Spirit.
They often manifest _____ of the _____ of the
person receiving the healing or miracle. (p. 186)

13. Sometimes, people will have an anointing for healing regarding a certain _____ of the
body or _____. (p. 186)

14. Gifts of miracles are the manifestation of the _____ power of God,
through the invasion of eternity into time. Because they override natural processes, miracles are
typically _____. (p. 187)

15. Miracle gifts are usually released when there is an _____ situation
or circumstance. (p. 187)

16. According to 1 Corinthians 14:3, what three benefits does the gift of prophecy bring to the church? (p. 187)

_____

_____

_____

17. Prophecy consists of both _____ (future events) and _____ (declaring the mind and counsel of God over a person or situation). (pp. 187, 189)

18. Discerning of spirits enables a believer to _____ or sense the _____ of angels, demons, the Holy Spirit, and human spirits. (p. 190)

19. The gift of discerning of spirits helps us to partner with heaven's agenda to see _____ on the earth. It also helps us to pray and exercise spiritual _____ over demonic powers. (p. 190)

20. The gift of divers kinds of tongues is a special endowment from the Holy Spirit that allows people to speak in _____ tongues or languages, especially as a _____ _____ in the church. The gift of various kinds of tongues can also refer to a situation in which a person becomes supernaturally fluent in _____ languages. (p. 191)

21. After a public discourse in an unknown tongue, the gift of interpretation—the _____ of the message into intelligible speech that edifies the people present—is much needed and powerful. (p. 193)

CONCLUSION

Just as the Holy Spirit bears fruit of various attributes in the lives of born-again believers (see Galatians 5:22–23), He also expresses different endowments or manifestations in the church. There is nothing in

Scripture that says the nine gifts listed in 1 Corinthians 12 are the only spiritual gifts, but they are definitely the starting point.

The Holy Spirit manifests supernatural endowments in order to bring the church together and create a beautiful symphony, with the different gifts working in concert for the benefit of all. We ought to honor the gifts within the church and the people to whom those gifts have been given. Every member is important, and every member deserves to be honored and appreciated. We honor the body by recognizing and honoring the gifts of the Spirit.

APPLYING PRINCIPLES OF THE MIRACULOUS

THINKING IT OVER

1. Consider these "Miracle Insights" questions from page 194 of *School of the Miraculous*:

    o What are the nine gifts of the Spirit listed in 1 Corinthians 12?

    o What did Paul say is the most important spiritual gift in the church?

    o What is the relationship between spiritual gifts and operating in the miraculous?

2. How have you seen the gifts of the Spirit in operation in your community of faith?

ACTING ON IT

1. Follow through with these "Practicum" exercises from page 195 of *School of the Miraculous*:

    o Which spiritual gift (or gifts) has God given you? How are you using it? How can you increase your use of this gift to build up others in the church and minister to those who do not yet know God? Seek God for other gifts He desires to give you, and begin to walk in them.

    o If you don't know which spiritual gift you have been given, ask God to reveal it to you by His Holy Spirit, the Gift Giver, and to help you grow in this gift as you continue to mature in Christlike character.

    o How is your particular gift necessary for the edification of the church? How can you better appreciate and honor the diverse gifts within the church and the individuals to whom they have been given? Make a point to express your appreciation to two people this week for exercising their gifts of the Spirit as the Lord leads them.

2. If you find you are jealous about someone else's spiritual gift or prideful about your own gift, confess this sin to God and receive His forgiveness. Ask Him to release you from the trap of comparing

yourself to others. Thank Him for all that He has given you and for the gifts He has given to others, for His eternal purposes.

PRAYING ABOUT IT

Father, in the name of Jesus, I thank You for who You are and all that You have done in my life. I recognize that You are the giver of good gifts, and all that is good and perfect comes from You. Therefore, I receive the gifts of the Spirit into my life. Through the Holy Spirit, I am empowered to operate in the supernatural. I thank You that the manifestation of Your Holy Spirit abounds in and through my life, enabling me to impact my world for the glory of God. Through the gifts of the Spirit, I tap into and release Your miraculous power. As You instruct us in 1 Corinthians 12:31, I earnestly pursue the best gifts so that I may be instrumental in edifying the body of Christ. In Matthew 7:7, Your Word says, *"Ask, and it shall be given you; seek, and you shall find; knock, and it shall be opened to you."* Therefore, I ask for all the gifts that I am able to receive and walk in. I pray this in the name of Jesus, amen!

MIRACLE TESTIMONY

A WORD OF KNOWLEDGE ABOUT HEALING

I accompanied Sid Roth on his Israel tour, and I was asked to speak at a large theater in Caesarea. The presence of God was so strong that you could feel it in the atmosphere. We began to worship God, and the glory came down. While we were in the glory realm, I spoke out that someone's eyes were being healed. There was a man in the audience who'd had double vision for as long as he could remember. When he caught the word of the Lord, he was instantly healed, and he has maintained his healing from that day.

A WORD OF KNOWLEDGE ABOUT RESTORATION

We received a written testimony from a woman who was watching when I was a guest on Sid Roth's program *It's Supernatural!* Her son had left home, saying that he would never return. The Lord gave me a word of knowledge about a prodigal son returning. I looked into the camera and said, "He is about to come home." This woman testified that the power of

God hit her. She began praying for her son, declaring that he would come home. Within seventy-two hours, the son came home, repented to his mother, and surrendered his life to God. Hallelujah!

ASK GOD TO USE YOU FOR HIS PURPOSES THROUGH THE PARTICULAR SPIRITUAL GIFTS HE HAS GIVEN YOU.

CHAPTER 13

THE SUPERNATURAL CHURCH

CHAPTER THEME

The church of the Lord Jesus Christ is a supernatural entity. When you remove God's supernatural power from the church, you don't have the church anymore; you merely have a religious organization.

If you are a member of the church of Jesus Christ, then you are a member of a supernatural community. When is the last time you tapped into the collective anointing of the church? This is God's plan for us! When the church embraces her true identity, we will see signs, wonders, and miracles. Never underestimate the power of unity in releasing the anointing.

QUESTIONS FOR REFLECTION

+ How would you define the church?

+ What are some common erroneous ideas about what the church is?

EXPLORING PRINCIPLES AND PURPOSES

1. The church is the _____ of Christ. (p. 199)

2. The church is a spiritual _____; it is alive. (p. 199)

3. The church is the full number of _____ (on earth and in heaven), as well as the local gathering of believers, transcending denominationalism. (p. 199)

4. The church is the supernatural _____ of God. (p. 199)

5. The church worldwide, or universal, is the collective gathering of God's people. We, the church, have been "_____ _____" of the world to _____ on behalf of the kingdom of God. (p. 199)

6. What do the Scriptures say happens when God's people gather together in unity? (p. 201)

   _____

   _____

   _____

7. The church was God's _____, not man's. Jesus Himself is the one who _____ and _____ the church, and He continues to build it to this day. (p. 201)

8. All believers—_____—are the church. And together, we are anointed to _____ into the territory of the enemy and _____ the regions of captivity that have been occupied by demonic powers, so that the culture of heaven can be established in those places. (p. 203)

9. Today, the church and individual believers are the _____ of God, because His Spirit dwells in us. (p. 204)

10. Christ not only delivered us from sin, but He also built the church according to the heavenly _____. (p. 204)

11. List the seven aspects of the heavenly pattern for the calling and work of the church: (p. 204)

_____

_____

_____

_____

_____

_____

_____

12. When the church reflects the _____ and _____ of heaven, then hell can't hinder its progress, and we can fulfill what God has called us to do. (p. 205)

13. Our churches must become houses of _____ for all nations. (p. 205)

14. We must see the _____ preached; people saved, healed, and delivered; and the dead _____ to life. People in the world need to see the power of God demonstrated in a real and tangible way. (p. 205)

15. Just as certain natural keys can unlock and lock doors, Jesus has given to the church _____ keys to unlock and lock situations in the earth. (p. 207)

16. What won't be released in the earthly realm until we utilize the supernatural keys that Christ has given us? (p. 207)

_____

_____

17. Miracles _____ the message of the cross, _____ the power of God, and _____ people to the King and His kingdom. (p. 207)

18. The church is responsible for _____ people with the knowledge of

God, becoming His instruments to fill the earth with His glory. (p. 209)

CONCLUSION

The church is built on the revelation of Jesus Christ. Every time we gather together in His name, the anointing for miracles, signs, and wonders is released. As a supernatural organism, the church has a supernatural foundation, meant to release supernatural power. The foundation determines the potential.

Today, the manifestation of the supernatural in the church is overdue! The church will be taken seriously when we accept and walk in the mandate Jesus gave us nearly two thousand years ago:

Go you therefore, and teach ["make disciples of" NIV] all nations, baptizing them in the name of the Father, and of the Son, and of the Holy Ghost: teaching them to observe all things whatsoever I have commanded you. —Matthew 28:19–20

We are to go into all the world and make disciples, teaching them to obey what Jesus has commanded. We have been commissioned by God to teach His supernatural ways to all nations.

APPLYING PRINCIPLES OF THE MIRACULOUS

THINKING IT OVER

1. Consider these "Miracle Insights" questions from page 211 of *School of the Miraculous*:
    o What does a supernatural church look like? What examples of a supernatural church do we see in Scripture?
    o What is the "collective anointing"? How do we tap into this anointing?
    o Recall the seven aspects of the heavenly pattern for the calling and work of the church. Does your church follow this pattern?
    o The Bible says that we are *"the light of the world."* What does this mean?

2. When the Israelites lived in the wilderness after their deliverance from Egypt, God instructed Moses on how to build the tabernacle, the place where the Lord would dwell with His people. Later, the tabernacle was replaced by the temple in Jerusalem. Why are the church and individual believers now referred to as God's temple?

ACTING ON IT

1. Jesus is the Light of the World, but we must yield ourselves to Him in order to release His light to the people around us. This week, say to Jesus, "I yield to You, Lord. Use me as a light to those around me."

2. Miracles authenticate the message of the cross, demonstrate the power of God, and draw people to the King and His kingdom. People all around us need to know the Lord. There is a family member who is waiting for you to embrace the full message of the kingdom and show them how real God is. There is a fellow employee waiting for you to demonstrate the power and love of Jesus in your job and in your personal life. Step out in faith to manifest God's kingdom on earth in obedience to His leading and in the power of His Spirit.

3. What is your outlook on attending and serving in a local church? Some Christians think they can serve God on their own, believing that their faith is solely an individual matter between themselves and God. Others feel that their past sins keep them from entering into fellowship with other believers. If you hold either of these mistaken views, renew your mind about the purpose of the church and your place in it from the principles in this chapter. Recognize that in God's plan, you need other believers and they need you. Accept His forgiveness for your sins and move forward in His purposes for your life. Begin to meet regularly with other believers for worship, prayer, teaching, and ministry. Discover the power of the blessed community!

PRAYING ABOUT IT

Father, in the name of Jesus, I thank You for who You are and all that You have done and continue to do in my life. In Your Word, the Lord Jesus declared that He will build His church, and the gates of hell will not prevail against it. Thank You for empowering Your people to be the *ekklesia* that You have called us to be. Thank You that we carry the legislative authority of the kingdom of God on earth. You are raising a generation of sons and daughters who operate in Your supernatural presence, power, and love—this is Your definition of a supernatural church. I declare that my church is a supernatural church and that we operate according to the heavenly pattern. Your kingdom is a kingdom of power; therefore, I declare that miracles, signs, and wonders are our portion. I walk in and release Your supernatural power daily. I declare that miracles are a natural part of my life and the lives of the people around me. Thank You for releasing Your anointing to destroy shackles of shame, guilt, condemnation, and fear. In the name of Jesus, amen!

MIRACLES OF HEALING

A little boy who came to our church couldn't speak, even though he was three years old. We prayed over him and declared that he would operate normally. After we prayed, he began to speak and function age-appropriately. We have seen a number of children on the spectrum be healed and begin to function normally, no matter what disorder they have been diagnosed with.

One person who attended a healing summit reported, "On April 26, 2018, I was at a weekend healing summit with Pastor Kynan and was healed of chronic migraine syndrome after nineteen years. Pastor also prophesied over me that another round of financial blessings would come into my life. In May 2018, my son got full-time work to help with our finances. *Amen* and *glory to God*."

ASK GOD TO STIR UP HIS CHURCH TO DEMONSTRATE HIS POWER IN TANGIBLE WAYS WITH HEALINGS, DELIVERANCES, AND SUPERNATURAL PROVISION.

CHAPTER 14

FIVE KEYS TO ACTIVATING GOD'S POWER

CHAPTER THEME

Many believers are equipped, but they are not activated. They have all the right "equipment"—they have the Word of God and the Holy Spirit—but they are not actively operating in God's supernatural purpose for their lives. To be activated to walk in daily miracles, it is imperative to follow these five spiritual practices: (1) submit, (2) obey, (3) expect, (4) stand, and (5) respond.

QUESTIONS FOR REFLECTION

+ Which principle in *School of the Miraculous* has been most significant for you? Why?

+ How can you be a doer of the Word and not just a hearer with regard to walking in the miraculous?

EXPLORING PRINCIPLES AND PURPOSES

1. To submit means to _____ _____ your own agenda so you can _____ and _____ to God's agenda. (p. 213)

2. We need to give the Holy Spirit room to _____ to us. (p. 214)

3. Do all that God instructs you to do in His _____ and by the leading of His
   _____. (p. 214)

4. Obedience to the Lord includes following established biblical _____ and
   divine _____. (p. 214)

5. Living in _____ that God will work signs, wonders, and miracles
   is like playing catch with your hands open, your eyes focused, your knees bent, and your body
   leaning forward, ready to receive the ball. (p. 214)

6. God is continuously _____ answers and manifestations and
   _____ life-changing encounters, so don't miss out! Stay ready! (p. 214)

7. Through what three ways can we remain in expectation and receive breakthroughs during our prayer
   times? (p. 215)

   _____

   _____

   _____

   _____

   _____

8. We need to stand firmly on the Word of God. When our faith is based on His Word, we can have
   _____ that He will intervene. (p. 215)

9. The more you _____ to God's leading, the more of His
   _____ you will see. (p. 216)

10. Every time we take a step of faith based on the revealed Word of God, we
_____ God's power in our lives. Without action, power remains merely
potential. (p. 216)

11. We must learn to move _____ according to the Word of God.
That is when something supernatural will happen! (p. 219)

12. Remember that prayer releases miracle power. In addition to praying in our own language, it is very
important that we make a consistent habit of praying in _____. Praying in the
_____ is one of the fastest ways to activate our spirit being. (p. 220)

CONCLUSION

God paid a tremendous price for us to have intimate fellowship with Him and walk in His miraculous power daily! No matter where you are in life or ministry, know that a lifestyle of miracles is possible. God has equipped you through the Holy Spirit, and He desires to activate you today to operate in a dimension that is beyond limitations. Miracles, signs, and wonders will become the norm in your life from this day forward!

APPLYING PRINCIPLES OF THE MIRACULOUS

THINKING IT OVER

1. Consider these "Miracle Insights" questions from page 221 of *School of the Miraculous*:
   o What are the five keys to activating God's power, and why are they important?
   o Share an example of submission to God from the Bible.
   o What can the woman with the issue of blood teach us about miracles?
   o What is the difference between being equipped and being activated?

2. God is continuously releasing answers and manifestations and offering life-changing encounters. How ready are you to receive them?

ACTING ON IT

1. Follow through with these "Practicum" exercises from page 222 of *School of the Miraculous*:

    o Consider the five keys to activating God's power: (1) submit, (2) obey, (3) expect, (4) stand, and (5) respond. Which of these keys are you in most need of working on? Decide today how you will specifically put this key into practice, and then follow through with it. Periodically review each of these keys to see if you are practicing them.

    o As you think about what you have learned in this book, list the ways in which God has equipped you to walk in the miraculous. Now list the areas in which you have actually been activated to move in the Spirit to see miracles daily. Which areas do you still need to initiate by believing God's Word and stepping out in faith? Move forward in activation so that you can daily walk in miracles!

    o Prayer is a secret power of the supernatural, and one of the ways in which we become activated in the miraculous. What priority do you currently place on prayer? Make a plan to pray regularly. Join with other believers at your church for prayer meetings. If there aren't any prayer meetings at your church, start one yourself with friends, family members, or other church members. Pray for each other's needs and the needs of your community. Ask God to demonstrate His power through your unified prayers that His kingdom would come and His will be done on earth as it is in heaven!

2. As you engage in heartfelt prayer based on God's Word, the Holy Spirit will give you revelation and emphasize specific promises from the Scriptures. He will send people to you, either to help you in some way or to be ministered to. He will highlight a word from your pastor or another preacher. The Holy Spirit will even speak to you in the middle of the day with instruction, caution, direction, and advice. You have to believe, receive, and take action on the words He gives. Has God given you a revelation or instruction that you have not yet acted on? Do so this week, remembering that without action, power remains merely potential.

PRAYING ABOUT IT

Father, in the name of Jesus, I thank You for who You are and all that You have done in my life. Today is a beautiful day. Today is a new opportunity to walk in Your presence and power. Everything that I need is found in You! By faith, I release Your power in and through my life. I activate the spiritual keys in Your Word that release the miraculous. I submit to the power of Your Word, obey Your precepts, stand on Your promises, and respond to Your divine instructions. I declare that I have been equipped to walk in the supernatural and experience all that You have purposed and predestined for my life. Nothing will separate me from the love of God in Christ Jesus! Every promise in Your Word is "yes and amen." Thank You for activating me in the supernatural, causing me to boldly operate in the culture of the miraculous. Miracles are commonplace through the power of Your presence. Thank You, Father, for moving in my life. In the name of Jesus, amen!

MIRACLE TESTIMONY

THE POWER OF PRAYER FOR DAILY MIRACLES

We can never overstate the power of prayer for daily walking in miracles. In fact, almost every miracle in the Bible was connected to a man or woman who prayed. It was through prayer that my wife and I began to experience miracles in our lives personally and through our ministry. Every Thursday night, we would meet for prayer in our living room and invite other people to come. And God would move in miraculous ways! One person who was barely able to walk was healed supernaturally. Scores of others were healed and delivered as well. Pretty soon, people from all over our city began to gather in our living room on Thursday evenings to enter into God's presence. Eventually, we needed to move to a larger room at a hotel, "and the rest is history" as our church was born.

REMEMBER THAT PRAYER IS A SECRET POWER OF THE SUPERNATURAL. AS YOU REGULARLY MEET WITH OTHER BELIEVERS FOR PRAYER, ASK GOD TO MOVE IN YOUR MIDST IN MIRACULOUS WAYS!

EXPLORING PRINCIPLES AND PURPOSES ANSWER KEY

CHAPTER 1

1. revelation

2. God manifests His supernatural power to show us that His agenda is infinitely more significant than our agenda.

3. Being "slain in the spirit" is an experience where the presence or anointing of God is so strong that it literally causes people to drop to the floor—without injury—and sometimes to appear unconscious. During this time, the Lord ministers to their spirit and emotions, manifesting His presence and bringing healing.

4. miracles; signs; wonders

5. "A sign, mark, token." The word can refer to "an unusual occurrence, transcending the common course of nature: of miracles and wonders by which God authenticates the men sent by him, or by which men prove that the cause they are pleading is God's."

6. "To follow after"; "so to follow one as to be always at his side"; "to follow close, accompany."

7. patterns; systems

8. The Bible clearly instructs us to seek first God's kingdom and righteousness in our lives. As we proclaim the kingdom, we activate the inevitable result: miracles.

9. When Jesus preached the kingdom, healings occurred, demons were evicted, people were set free from oppression, and miracles happened!

10. follow

11. (1) Satan's kingdom of darkness will be cast out and demonic powers will be subdued. (2) Believers will be given the ability to speak with new languages, either heavenly or earthly tongues. (3) Believers will experience divine protection. (4) The sick will be healed supernaturally.

12. This is the belief that the message of the cross—forgiveness for sin—is enough. Because the gospel of exclusion essentially ignores the glorious implications of Christ's resurrection, it is a powerless message in terms of living the kingdom lifestyle.

13. eyes; earth; strong; heart; perfect

14. dynamite

15. demonstration

16. Holy Spirit

17. baptism

18. Release; Instigate; Stand; Keep

CHAPTER 2

1. "the domain of the king"

2. (1) conquest; (2) colonization

3. rulership; dominion

4. settling among; establishing control over

5. kingship; authority; influence; government

6. The kingdom of God is characterized by righteousness, peace, and joy in the Holy Spirit.

7. *righteousness*: God's right way of doing things. Justice, judgment, and morality.

   peace: shalom, or completeness. Nothing missing and nothing broken.

   joy: a state of being that is void of fear, worry, anxiety, or shame.

8. usurped; Satan

9. regain; restore

10. colonize

11. ambassadors; empowered; release

12. We are like earthen vessels containing treasure. (See 2 Corinthians 2:7.) God wants His kingdom to be established within us.

13. us; earth

14. We experience the demonstration of the kingdom by yielding to the government of God in our lives.

15. proof

16. Every single believer has been called and commissioned to release God's kingdom wherever they go.

17. available

18. ability; desire

19. When we surrender to God, we are telling Him that He has the right to direct our lives.

20. submit; recipients

CHAPTER 3

1. It means that we are citizens of a heavenly kingdom that has a distinct culture, and we must become infused with that culture if we want to live the Christian life successfully.

2. supernatural

3. language; customs

4. "A system of communication used by a particular country or community"

5. faith

6. declare

7. We are telling Him that He is not as powerful as He claims to be.

8. Word

9. make; grant; done

10. greater; greater

11. "A traditional and widely accepted way of behaving or doing something that is specific to a particular society, place, or time"

12. holiness

13. We are made holy through the blood of Jesus alone. His holiness and righteousness are imputed to us by faith. We receive holiness as a gift. Holiness cannot be conjured up, or acquired, by our own strength.

14. yielding

15. abstain

16. spiritual power; influence

17. Another vital aspect of the customs of God's kingdom is the practice of showing honor. Like faith, honor is a currency of the kingdom.

18. To honor is to highly esteem or attach value to someone or something.

19. "weight" or "glory"

20. catalyst; presence; glory

21. respect; release

CHAPTER 4

1. *"You are the Christ, the Son of the living God"* (Matthew 16:16).

2. *"You are Peter [Petros, Greek], and upon this rock I will build My church; and the gates of hell shall not prevail against it"* (Matthew 16:18).

3. characteristics; who; what

4. spirit-man

5. up close; personal

6. God wanted Adam to see Him right away when he came alive so that God would be the image all human beings would look to for their identity.

7. Christ

8. The devil wants people in an identity crisis because if you don't know who you are, you cannot walk in the authority that comes with that identity. Additionally, the devil detests the image of God, and every time he sees us, he is reminded of the Creator Himself.

9. receive; born; DNA; supernatural

10. transformation

11. The term "new creature" signifies "a new kind of being that has been recently transformed."

12. incorruptible

13. are

14. sons; daughters

15. We are able to walk in and release the supernatural.

16. Source

17. connection; communion

18. in; through

19. peace; peace

20. The consciousness we must walk in for our lives is the separation of light from darkness and the removal of chaos.

21. confidence

22. love

23. I receive from my spiritual inheritance, and I live according to it.

24. forget; consciousness; reality

25. lie; stop; broken

CHAPTER 5

1. honoring; experiencing

2. unapproachable

3. approached

4. light; within

5. filled

6. I should think of miracles as something I release.

7. atmosphere; perceivable

8. blood; Holy Spirit

9. lifestyle; dwelling

10. house; people

11. carriers

12. convey

13. There are people who will never receive what God intends for them.

14. sensitive; prompts

15. awaiting

CHAPTER 6

1. "To conform one's self (i.e. one's mind and character) to another's pattern, (fashion one's self according to)."

2. *"Love not the world"* isn't a reference to the physical planet or the people in it, but rather to the fallen world system that operates on the earth. This system is governed by *"the lust of the flesh, and the lust of the eyes, and the pride of life"* (1 John 2:15–16). To love the world is not just to participate in sinful activities, such as illicit sex, drugs, or violence. It also includes possessing a "worldly" mind-set. To think like the world and embrace its ideas is just as much loving the world as committing any of the "big" sins we can conceive of.

3. feel; experience

4. see

5. vanity

6. sin; senses

7. governed

8. We must be transformed in our priorities and thinking.

9. spiritual mind-set

10. Word; Spirit

11. mind, yield; challenge

12. Every time we renew our mind, we gain access to greater dimensions of God's glory and power.

13. enemy; deceived

14. paradigm; positions

15. capacity

16. (1) they are not walking in biblical faith; (2) they are suffering from a weakness of faith

17. measure of faith

18. faith; unbelief

19. read; speak; meditate

20. works; greater works

CHAPTER 7

1. "A clear declaration of something" and "a public or official announcement dealing with a matter of great importance"

2. words; Word

3. deemed unlawful; deemed lawful

4. negative; adverse

5. deeper

6. We were created by God to govern on earth through our words.

7. words; world

8. A physical hand can be an instrument of construction, but it can also be a weapon of destruction. It depends on how a person uses it. The same is true of the tongue. Our words can either build or destroy.

9. license

10. faith-filled

11. proclaiming; statements

12. intentionality

13. Intercession

14. think; say

15. proclamation; alignment

CHAPTER 8

1. abide

2. anointed

3. oil

4. "An unguent or smearing, i.e. the special endowment ("chrism") of the Holy Spirit"

5. call of God; aroma

6. heaven

7. yokes; burdens

8. (1) The anointing is tangible. (2) The anointing is transferable.

9. felt

10. conveyed

11. faith; obedience

12. When I obey the assignment God has placed upon my life, I will see the manifestation of the anointing in and through me.

13. acting on

14. increase

15. caught

16. In *School of the Miraculous, surrender* is used in the context of yielding to God and ceasing to resist Him.

17. yield

CHAPTER 9

1. bashfulness; insecurity; timidity; feelings of intimidation; nervousness; anxiety; a paralyzing incapacity

2. manipulate; corrupt; trapped

3. love

4. fear; faith

5. false

6. presence; power; protection

7. natural and unnatural fears

8. remaining; spiritually; emotionally; mentally; physically

9. authority

10. In the natural world, a stronghold is "a place that has been fortified so as to protect it against attack." Strongholds are often used by armies during warfare. In the spiritual world, it is much the same, except that these fortresses are occupied by demonic powers.

11. The devil establishes strongholds in people's lives so he can steal their joy and rob them of the purpose and plan of God.

12. truth; power

13. deceitful arguments; false images

14. spirit

15. faith; fear

16. lie

17. stagnation; weakened

18. empowered

19. boldness and audacity

20. expression

21. Creator

CHAPTER 10

1. within; out

2. instruments; One

3. staying

4. awakening

5. "A coming into awareness"

6. An awareness of who we are in Christ and of the Spirit who resides within us

7. face-to-face

8. dominion; intimacy; obedience

9. God's original design and purpose for creating us

10. separated; restore

11. opposition

12. An awareness and sensitivity to God's presence; feeling as if one is literally walking with God; basking in God's presence instead of worrying about one's needs, frailties, or failures (answers may vary slightly)

13. Focusing more on one's frailties and failures than on God; being more concerned about other people's opinions than about God (answers may vary slightly)

14. personal awakening

15. The Holy Spirit

CHAPTER 11

1. manifestation

2. prayer

3. perceive

4. The more we tap into the supernatural power of God

5. Sin

6. bitterness; resentment; forgive

7. We are not walking in love and our faith is not working.

8. expect; power; provision

9. measure

10. The only way we can pray without ceasing is to pray in the Holy Spirit.

11. tongues; strengthens

12. renew; mind of Christ

13. supernatural; natural

14. Through intercession

15. hearing

16. inheritance

CHAPTER 12

1. manifestations; edification

2. word of wisdom; word of knowledge; faith; gifts of healing; working of miracles; prophecy; discerning of spirits; divers (various) kinds of tongues; interpretation of tongues

3. diverse

4. appreciate; jealous; prideful

5. important

6. witnesses

7. the present or the future

8. feeling; impression; spoken

9. hearer; speaker

10. believe

11. The gift of miracles

12. independent; faith

13. part; disease

14. *dunamis*; instantaneous

15. impossible

16. edification; exhortation; comfort

17. foretelling; forth-telling

18. recognize; presence

19. miracles; authority

20. various; public discourse; heavenly

21. translation

CHAPTER 13

1. body

2. organism

3. believers

4. institution

5. called out; convene

6. The anointing flows

7. idea; identified; established

8. collectively; advance; liberate

9. temple

10. pattern

11. preach the kingdom; demonstrate the power of God; call people to repentance; make disciples; continue in prayer, the Word, and fellowship; walk in love; repeat steps 1–6.

12. glory; power

13. prayer

14. gospel; raised

15. spiritual

16. Certain heavenly blessings and provisions

17. authenticate; demonstrate; draw

18. illuminating

CHAPTER 14

1. lay aside; listen; respond

2. speak

3. Word; Spirit

4. patterns; principles

5. expectation

6. releasing; offering

7. (1) be in total agreement with our fellow intercessors; (2) pray fervently; (3) take time to wait on the Lord, asking, "Lord, speak to me"

8. confidence

9. respond; glory

10. activate

11. purposefully

12. tongues; Spirit

ABOUT THE AUTHOR

Dr. Kynan T. Bridges is the senior pastor of Grace & Peace Global Fellowship in Tampa, Florida. With a profound revelation of the Word of God and a dynamic teaching ministry, Dr. Bridges has revolutionized the lives of many in the body of Christ. Through his practical approach to applying the deep truths of the Word of God, he reveals the authority and identity of the new covenant believer.

God has placed on Dr. Bridges a particular anointing for understanding and teaching the Scriptures, along with the gifts of prophecy and healing. Dr. Bridges and his wife, Gloria, through an apostolic anointing, are committed to equipping the body of Christ to live in the supernatural every day and to fulfill the Great Commission. It is the desire of Dr. Bridges to see the nations transformed by the unconditional love of God.

A highly sought speaker and published author of a number of books, his previous books with Whitaker House include *Invading the Heavens*, *Unmasking the Accuser*, *The Power of Prophetic Prayer*, and *Kingdom Authority*. Dr. Bridges is a committed husband, a mentor, and a father of five beautiful children: Ella, Naomi, Isaac, Israel, and Anna.

Welcome to Our House!

We Have a Special Gift for You

It is our privilege and pleasure to share in your love of Christian books. We are committed to bringing you authors and books that feed, challenge, and enrich your faith.

To show our appreciation, we invite you to sign up to receive a specially selected **Reader Appreciation Gift**, with our compliments. Just go to the Web address at the bottom of this page.

God bless you as you seek a deeper walk with Him!

WE HAVE A GIFT FOR YOU. VISIT:

whpub.me/nonfictionthx

WHITAKER
HOUSE